What Others Are Saying About
Dave Jetson and *Setting True Boundaries*

"In *Setting True Boundaries*, Dave Jetson tackles one of the most important topics within the change process with clarity and impact. He has always delivered content in a unique, honest, and inspiring way and scores again with this must read on boundaries. Boundaries are a universal struggle for all relationships, and Dave provides a roadmap toward creating stronger relationships with those closest to us."

— Miles Adcox, Owner and CEO of Onsite Workshops

"Dave Jetson's view of the importance of boundaries is an important approach to authentic communication. He draws the reader into learning about boundaries and then gives them clear examples of how boundaries play out in case histories. All of us will improve our relationships with ourselves and with others through reading *Setting True Boundaries*. I recommend this book."

— Sharon Wegscheider-Cruse, Founder of Onsite Workshops, Family Therapist, and Author of *Becoming a Sage*

"Dave Jetson's book has given me the ability to see myself and my life in a completely new way and that has given me the chance to make real, lasting changes. I have found relief and real *healing* in so many of the relationships I have struggled with for so long. I think everyone needs to read this book."

— Patrick Snow, Publishing Coach and International Bestselling Author of *Creating Your Own Destiny* and *Boy Entrepreneur*

"After serving as a mental health therapist for forty-plus years, I thought I knew a lot about boundaries. But Dave Jetson's book, *Setting True Boundaries: How to Create Respect, Safety, and Freedom in Relationships*, opened a new depth of thought about the subject for me. I was able to look beyond the surface of boundaries, explore how to set firm limits, continue to monitor them, and enforce them with compassion. Dave provides many practical examples that show how setting effective boundaries grows relationships. The most satisfying thing about reading this book was going to work the next day with new insight to skillfully help my clients set effective boundaries."

— James Gardiner, PhD, Licensed Psychologist, and
Neuropsychologist

"We hear so many talk about the necessity of establishing safe boundaries in our relationships. But in *Setting True Boundaries*, Dave Jetson clearly explains the essential components of an effective boundary, and shows, with clarifying examples, how they work to restore respect and bring healing to troubled relationships."

— Jim Munro, Bioethics Consultant, Dunedin, Florida

"While the concept of boundaries is not new, Dave's presentation gives fresh and practical perspectives. It has reminded me of some new areas of life in which I need to work on setting boundaries. As a recovering nice guy, it is time to take my boundary setting in a more positive direction before it comes out 'sideways' as Dave likes to say."

— Ed Coambs MBA, MA, CFP®, LMFT, Founder of Carolinas
Couples Counseling and Leader in Financial Therapy

"This powerful book gives you the tools needed to understand and approach setting and enforcing boundaries, particularly with unhealthy or toxic people in your life who like to exert their control. You'll even learn the best ways to protect your time and energy for the things that matter most."

— Susan Friedmann, CSP, and International Bestselling Author of
Riches in Niches: How to Make it BIG in a small market

"Learning to set boundaries changed my life. Now Dave Jetson walks readers through the practical steps to setting effective boundaries that will help them transform their relationships from dysfunctional to respectful and loving. *Setting True Boundaries* is a book we all need."

— Tyler R. Tichelaar, PhD and Award-Winning Author of
Narrow Lives and *When Teddy Came to Town*

"In *Setting True Boundaries*, Dave Jetson reveals the truth that setting boundaries enhances relationships. Boundaries show respect to both the person setting the boundary and the person whose behavior needs to be curbed. Dave's practical advice on how to set these boundaries makes it easy and effective. Everyone in any kind of relationship— which means everyone—needs to read this book."

— Nicole Gabriel, Author of *Finding Your Inner Truth* and
Stepping Into Your Becoming

"I learned more about boundaries in the introduction of this book than I have in twenty-five years of therapy, workshops, and Twelve-Step groups."

— Rick Kahler, MSFP, CFP

"What's beautiful about this book is that it will help create *sustainable* change in setting boundaries. Dave doesn't just give superficial advice on how to create boundaries; instead, he focuses on helping the reader identify the underlying beliefs, fears, and anxieties that need to be addressed before any real changes will take place. I will definitely be recommending this book to all my clients, but also to my friends and family because we can all use a refresher in healthy boundaries!"

— Megan McCoy, PhD, LMFT, Professor of Practice in Personal Financial Planning, Director of Personal Financial Planning Masters Program, Kansas State University

"Dave Jetson's book *Setting Boundaries* is an evolutionary new look at communicating boundaries in a safe and non-harmful way. If enough people read this book, it could actually change the paradigm of domestic and societal violence. This very well could be the most profound abuse recovery book ever written."

— Valerie Harper, Business Consultant, Scottsdale, Arizona

"This wonderful, eye-opening book is a gift to anyone who reads it. It completely changed my understanding of boundaries and how they work. My important relationships have improved significantly. Seeing boundaries in a new way has allowed me to feel less stress and experience more joy each day."

— Erik C. Milam, CFP

"Victor Frankl once said, 'There is a space between stimulus and response, and in that space is the power to choose!' Dave Jetson has brilliantly outlined the power of choice in *Setting True Boundaries*. In so doing, he has also given us a loving and compassionate way forward in building strong and respectful relationships within ourselves and with those we love. Another title for this book might be "Adulting 101: How Modeling True Boundaries Co-Creates Better Human Beings and Happier Lives."

— Neal Van Zutphen, M.S., CFP®, FBS®, CRPC®

"The examples in Dave Jetson's *Setting True Boundaries* are powerful because they are practical. Jetson's step-by-step (and introspective) guidance for how to develop and implement boundaries in a variety of settings and relationships—parents, spouses, friends, colleagues, clients—is a beneficial read for us all."

— Meghaan Lurtz, PhD, PFP/Financial Therapy

"Dave Jetson's *Setting True Boundaries* is a deep dive into a topic most therapists hope to address but few have been fully equipped to cover. The detail with which Dave addresses true boundaries enables me as a therapist to have confidence in the subject matter without fear that my clients will suffer if we don't fully address it all in one session. Also, the questions at the end of each section make the material practical and easier to access, review, and address any time someone feels challenged in maintaining their own boundaries, especially me. Thanks, Dave. I highly recommend this work for everyone."

— Adam Petty, Principal Counselor, Sound Healing Arts LLC

"If you're looking for a book to provide tools to identify, develop, and implement healthy boundaries and limits in a very eloquent and honoring way, this is it! The book has numerous examples, questions, and scenarios that are pertinent and written in an easy-to-understand format. I was even able to get my kids onboard. It beautifully complements personal growth endeavors!"

— Alison Scherr, MS

"Dave Jetson's work on boundaries is a valuable and detailed guide for people on how to establish and maintain healthy perimeters in relationships. He walks through many real-life examples of circumstances and the process to think through and solve the question of boundary-setting. Dave's reflections at the end of each chapter are an excellent review of the concepts covered in the chapter. With helpful charts and exercises for each topic, readers can construct every aspect of healthy boundaries they need to guide their way to more fulfilling and respectful relationships."

— Susan Zimmerman, ChFC, LMFT, Chartered
Financial Consultant, LMFT

"*Setting True Boundaries* is an insightful and practical guide on how to do the complex work of setting effective boundaries in your life. A must read for parents, practitioners, and anyone interested in living a more empowered and joyful life."

— Kathleen Burns Kingsbury, Wealth Psychology Expert
and Author of *Breaking Money Silence*®

SETTING
TRUE
BOUNDARIES

How to Create Respect, Safety, and Freedom in Relationships

A book of support

Dave Jetson, MS

AVIVA
PUBLISHING
New York

Setting True Boundaries: How to Create Respect, Safety, and Freedom in Relationships

Published by:
Aviva Publishing
Lake Placid, NY
(518) 523-1320
www.AvivaPubs.com

Dave Jetson
www.jetsoncounseling.com
www.livingtrueinc.com
jetsond@yahoo.com

Disclaimer: The examples in this book are designed to give clarity to the boundary process. While many of them are based on true stories, names and situations have been modified to maintain the confidentiality of the people involved.

ISBN: 978-1-947937-27-7
Library of Congress Control Number:
Editor: Tyler Tichelaar, Superior Book Productions
Cover and Interior Book Design: Nicole Gabriel, Angel Dog Productions
Author Photo Credit: Johnny Sundby

Every attempt has been made to source properly all quotes.
Printed in the United States of America

"You get what you tolerate."

— Henry Cloud

DEDICATION

To my clients who taught me the importance of true boundaries and the positive changes that occur when they are put into practice.

To all my children and grandchildren who have been my greatest teachers. I love all of you.

To my wife, Liz. Your love, understanding, support, and encouragement have helped keep me on track. Thank you.

To God who has guided me every step of the way. The thoughts, patterns, and scriptural validations you have inspired me with have made this book. I praise you for the many blessings you have given in this book as well as the understanding that has allowed me to implement true boundaries in my life.

Acknowledgments

Almost everything in life is achieved with the love and support of friends and family. I could not have come to this place in my life and in my career without my family, faith, and the clients who have both encouraged and inspired me. Special thanks are due to:

My wife, Liz, who has been my undying champion.

My children and grandchildren, who have taught and challenged me while perpetually believing in me.

Each and every client who has bravely shared their personal story.

Kathleen Fox, who applied her tremendous writing and authorship talent to my ideas.

Tyler Tichelaar, for his editing skills.

Nicole Gabriel, for designing the book cover.

Jaclyn Lanae, who helped pull the elements together.

Patrick Snow, for being my coach and guiding me through the publishing process.

Josh Jetson, for his marketing advice and expertise.

Ashley Auwerter, for her own marketing efforts.

And above all else, to God who guided my every thought and word in bringing these concepts to the public.

Contents

"When you feel yourself becoming angry, resentful, or exhausted, pay attention to where you haven't set a healthy boundary."

— Crystal Andrus

INTRODUCTION

"Daring to set boundaries is about having
the courage to love ourselves…."

— Brené Brown

Imagine you're at a basketball game. It's being held in a typical gym,
with a basket at each end of the floor. There are the usual tiers of seats
for spectators and the usual players out on the court. But something
isn't quite right. There are no lines on the floor. No referees are out there
with the players. None of the boundaries is marked, and there is no one
to enforce the rules.

In this game, there is no such thing as out of bounds. If a ball bounces
off the floor and into the stands, the players charge after it, leaping over
the seats or falling into the laps of cringing spectators. One of the fans
might grab the ball and throw it back onto the court, doing his best to
get it back into the possession of whichever team he supports. Some
fans might even try to make a basket themselves. Players run with the
ball like football quarterbacks, wrestle for the ball, knock each other
down, and throw wildly at whichever basket is closer. No one knows
where the free-throw line is, and it doesn't matter because there are no
referees to call penalties.

After only a few minutes of play, the spectators in the front rows have moved to higher tiers where they feel safer. The players are exhausted, bruised, and battered. Their competitive spirit has soured into anger. The game has turned into a free-for-all. Which team is ahead is anyone's guess, since no one knows the rules. There's just one thing that both the players and the fans know for sure: This game is no fun.

Chaos like this is what can happen when we operate with no boundaries.

The lack of boundaries in this example is not simply about the missing lines on the playing floor. Confusion over the exact location of the free-throw lines or the edges of the court is more a symptom of having no boundaries than a cause. The real boundaries in an athletic event are not the markings on the court but the rules of the game; the markings are merely reminders of those rules.

It's common, in discussing boundaries, to compare them to lines like the ones that mark the limits of basketball courts. Even more common analogies are walls, fences, or borders. We're used to thinking of boundaries in terms of protecting or defining physical or psychological space. In this view, a boundary is focused on keeping something or someone in or out. "This is my space over here, that is your space over there, and don't you dare cross the line into my territory without my permission."

This analogy isn't quite accurate. Whether we're talking about sports, organizations, or families, boundaries are not about space. They are about behavior.

To illustrate, suppose that four of the spectators at our basketball game are a family: Mr. and Mrs. Muddle and their daughter and son. They find the chaos of the game quite familiar because its lack of boundaries reflects the lack of boundaries in their lives. Day-to-day life at the Muddle house looks something like this:

The children have no set bedtimes and no limits on television or video games, so most nights they stay up late and fall asleep on the couch, often while watching a program filled with violence or other inappropriate content. Mornings are a madhouse, with everyone tired and stressed as they try to get out of the house for work and school. The children rarely get their homework done or remember to take it to school. Mealtimes and menus are haphazard, with everyone snacking at random without regard for nutrition. As a result, everyone in the family is susceptible to colds and other illnesses.

Mom and Dad argue, struggle for power, and manipulate each other. The children don't have any idea what behavior is expected of them until they do something their parents don't like. Then they are yelled at and threatened, but there is no explanation of what they are supposed to do, no consequences, and no opportunity to learn from their experiences. If the kids act disrespectfully, their parents sometimes punish them harshly, sometimes ignore them, and sometimes laugh at them.

All the family members use each other's things, from toothbrushes to computers to cars, without asking. They steal from each other's wallets or piggy banks and barge into bathrooms and bedrooms without knocking. Toys, tools, and electronics are routinely lost or broken, which leads to accusations and shouting, but doesn't result in anyone taking better care of their belongings. Laundry, trash, and dirty dishes pile up. Communication is marked by yelling, blaming, manipulating, gossiping, lying, and interrupting.

There is no consistency, no safety, and no respect in the Muddle household. No one in the family likes living this way. They all feel stressed, powerless, and angry. In order to change their pattern of disorder and disrespect, they need to learn how to create and follow through with true boundaries.

True boundaries are about taking action to create trust, safety, and re-

spect for both yourself and others. You build self-respect by acknowl-
edging your need for a limit and honoring yourself enough to set one.
Boundaries build respect for you, the recipient of the boundary, because you create a pattern where you do not need to get angry or be
disrespectful to the other person. You do not attempt to control them;
you modify your own behavior.

Creating boundaries does not mean telling someone, "You can't do
that," or "You have to do this." You don't have that kind of control over
another person's behavior. Instead, true boundaries are about both positive and negative consequences. Consequences are actions that directly relate to a situation that has no emotional response associated with
it. Boundaries are about modifying your behavior in response to the
consequence the other person is choosing by their behavior. "If you do
this, I will do that." You focus on the only behavior you can control—
your own.

A true boundary creates safety for the person setting it, builds respect
between both parties, is emotionally neutral rather than escalating anger or other emotions, and fosters increased closeness and understanding. True boundaries include these three components:

1. *A limit.* This is what the person setting the boundary wants or
   doesn't want; it defines what is and is not acceptable behavior. In
   sports, this is clearly stated in the rules. "A free throw must be made
   from behind the free throw line" is a limit. In relationships, it is up
   to the person setting the limit to clearly communicate it. "I need
   you to let me know if you won't be home in time for dinner" is a
   limit.

2. *Consequences—both positive and negative.* It's important that the
   consequences specify the positive consequence that will happen if
   the limit is respected as well as the negative consequence that will
   happen if it is not. Again, in sports these limits are clearly estab-

lished up front. "If you make your free throw from behind the line, the shot counts and play continues" is a positive consequence. "If you make your free throw from ahead of the line, the shot doesn't count" is a negative consequence.

In relationships, the consequences need to be clearly spelled out. "If you let me know you're going to be late, I'll wait for you and we can have dinner together" is a positive consequence. "If you don't let me know you're going to be late, the kids and I will eat, and you can make your own dinner when you get home" is a negative consequence.

3. *Consistent enforcement and follow-through.* In sports, consistent enforcement and follow-through is relatively easy; it's part of the game's structure. Players who violate the game's rules will be penalized. This doesn't happen randomly; it's consistent and fair, in order to protect the game's integrity. Protecting the integrity of our relationships requires the same fairness and consistency. This is the hardest part about boundaries. When you set limits with other people, you need to follow through with the consequences every time there is compliance or a violation. If you follow through with a consequence ninety-nine times, but fail to do so the hundredth time, the boundary has been broken and will need to be reestablished.

All of these components of a true boundary are about behavior, not space.

Yes, the lines on a basketball court mark out physical spaces. But the lines' real purpose is to remind people of the game's rules, which are the true boundaries. The free-throw line isn't a barrier that physically prevents a player from standing too close to the basket to shoot a free throw. Instead, it's a reminder of the rule that says, "If you stand closer than this line and make your free throw, the penalty is that it won't count." The line is merely a symbol of the behavior expected and the consequence spelled out in the rules.

As long as no one violates the rules, the game continues. When someone does violate a rule, the game is interrupted while the referees enforce the appropriate consequences. The officials don't have the power to compel players to do or not do anything. Referees don't physically stop players from violating rules. Instead, they enforce the penalties established by the rules.

Obviously, referees do sometimes make mistakes. At any given time, for example, they may not be in the right place to see a boundary violation clearly or even to notice that one has occurred. They can't impose penalties for infractions they aren't aware of.

And since officials are human, they may not always succeed at keeping their emotions out of their decisions, even though they are trained to stay neutral. If players, coaches, or fans get angry over a particular ruling or a rules violation, the referees might occasionally get angry or defensive as well. When this happens, the result is often a larger penalty, such as a technical foul, that is a punishment rather than a consequence. Generally, such a penalty escalates everyone's emotions, which could result in even more fouls and make it harder for the game to continue.

Still, in sports, the ideal—and the reality, most of the time—is that the referees consistently and fairly enforce the rules. They are neutral third parties whose role is not to support either team. They aren't emotionally invested in which team wins or loses. Instead, their loyalty is to the rules and the game itself. This neutral position supports their authority and helps ensure that the players respect their decisions. True boundaries help create an emotionally neutral position by allowing the other person to freely choose the consequences of their behavior and allowing you to follow through with their choice of consequences with no need to control or direct the outcome.

In addition to this consistent enforcement, another aspect of boundaries in sports is that everyone knows what they are ahead of time. The rules don't change from game to game. Neither do the penalties for violating those rules. Players might object to certain rulings from time to time or complain that they have been victims of a bad call, but they can't say they are taken by surprise. The penalty for a foul is the same in this week's game as it was last week or last month. Everyone knows what to expect.

Life, of course, isn't a game like basketball. Setting boundaries with other people is a lot more complicated than learning the rules of a game. But there are similarities. In sports, the boundaries are meant to create safety, consistency, and integrity. The rules help prevent physical injuries, ensure that wins and losses are fair and legitimate, and provide a structure to help people understand the game. They ensure that a game is a fair and enjoyable contest rather than a free-for-all.

In relationships, boundaries create emotional (and sometimes physical) safety, build respect, and help people understand each other and enjoy the relationship. With true boundaries, both parties are free to be themselves in the relationship as they interact with mutual respect.

Introduction Reflections

True boundaries are about choices and consequences. While you may have not been taught true boundaries, that does not mean you cannot learn to set and follow through with them. Before you start the process of setting true boundaries in your life, it is important to ask yourself, "What relationship patterns do I want to change and which ones do I not want to change at this time?"

While you have the right to set the limits in your life with true boundaries for creating more safety and respect, you may choose not to set those limits in certain areas with certain relationships. This book's purpose is to help you decide which relationships are creating enough tension and stress that you want to create a change in them.

Once you choose in which areas, if any, you wish to create more safety and respect, the consequences will start to play out. That means you will get the same results you have in the past for the areas where you do not wish to set boundaries. The areas where you wish to set boundaries have consequences and follow-through that create a different outcome, which is what this book is about.

At the end of each chapter will be reflection questions and exercises to help you create the framework for true boundaries. After you complete this book and the exercises, you will have boundaries that can be implemented in your life. You have the option of exploring as many or as few boundaries as you wish. If you are wanting to establish just one boundary, it is important that it is a boundary you can be successful with. If the boundary is very difficult and you do not have other easier boundaries in place, creating it successfully may be much more challenging.

You may want to respond to the reflection questions in writing in a notebook or computer document so that, at the completion of the book, you will have written out boundaries with consequences to give the person you intend to set boundaries with. With the tools in place, it is time to reflect and respond to the questions.

What is your definition of a boundary?

_____

_____

_____

Who taught you what a boundary is?

_____

_____

_____

Who taught you how to challenge a boundary?

_____

_____

_____

In which relationships do you feel safe and respected to the point there is no need for change at this time?

_____

_____

_____

In what relationships do you feel unsafe and/or disrespected to the point you would like to create positive change?

_____

_____

_____

List the boundaries you have created or attempted to create in the past:

_____

_____

_____

_____

_____

Which of the attempted boundaries created a successful outcome, meaning the other person complied without any form of tension?

_____

_____

_____

Which of the established boundaries do you continue to have success with?

_____

_____

_____

Which boundaries were not successful?

_____

_____

_____

CHAPTER ONE

WHAT WE DON'T KNOW ABOUT TRUE BOUNDARIES

*"Boundaries represent awareness, knowing what limits are
and then respecting those limits."*

— David W. Earle

In sports, new players don't automatically know the rules and boundaries. Someone has to teach them the game's rules, as well as the etiquette and expectations that define appropriate behavior in that sport. For a first-hand demonstration of this, all you have to do is watch a group of five-year-olds play their first tee-ball game. Most of the fledgling athletes know something about the basics of hitting and catching the ball, but when it comes to the game itself, they don't have a clue what they're doing. They might run bases the wrong way, forget which team they're on, or wrestle their team-mates for possession of the ball. They have to be taught the rules and boundaries that govern how the game is played.

In the same way, all of us need to learn about boundaries in relationships. Many people have no real idea what boundaries are.

Very few of us, as children, are taught about healthy true boundaries. We don't learn how to set true boundaries for ourselves or how to respect the boundaries of others. Instead, many of us are taught bullying, punishment, manipulation, enmeshment, and shame. Punishments are actions imposed on another person as a way of control and are administered with heightened feelings that elevate the response. This is especially true for those who grow up with addiction, abuse, or other forms of dysfunction. Some of us are treated with such disrespect that we are actively taught not to set boundaries. We don't learn to respect ourselves, and instead, are taught to believe we aren't valuable and important enough to be treated respectfully. We grow up assuming we don't even have the right to set boundaries. It's not surprising, then, that many adults don't have a clear understanding of what boundaries are.

To create and follow through with true boundaries takes dedicated practice. Athletes discipline themselves to be good at their sport by the discipline of practice. Boundaries are a form of discipline. True boundaries are created for increased trust, safety, and respect for ourselves and the people around us. True boundaries are a form of self-love and a love for others. As Hebrews 12:5-6 states, discipline is good for us: "My son, do not disdain the discipline of the Lord or lose heart when reproved by him; for whom the Lord loves, he disciplines."

Behavior That Violates True Boundaries

Before you can successfully set true boundaries, you need to learn what boundaries are. Even more important, you need to learn to value yourself enough to understand that you are precious and worthy of safety, comfort, and respect. Only then can you set true boundaries that teach others to treat you with the respect everyone deserves.

One of the first things to understand about boundaries, then, is what they are and when they are being violated. Any time people treat you disrespectfully, they may be violating your boundaries. The following list includes just a few examples of behavior that violates boundaries. If the people on the receiving end have not been taught to respect and value themselves, they won't even necessarily recognize that the behaviors are violations.

- Children disobeying rules that parents have set.

- A boss who yells, swears, threatens, or otherwise treats employees disrespectfully.

- Parents, spouses, siblings, or children who yell, swear, threaten, or otherwise treat family members disrespectfully.

- A spouse who spends joint money on himself or herself without consulting the other partner.

- A family member or roommate who leaves unreasonable amounts of clutter in joint spaces, doesn't do an agreed-upon share of chores, or uses others' things without permission.

- Physical abuse—hitting, slapping, and spanking, as well as less violent touching such as unwelcome tickling.

- Sexual abuse, in its entire range from inappropriate remarks or sexual behavior or remarks in the workplace to the violent rape of a small child.

- Verbal abuse, such as negative name calling, belittling, swearing at, threatening, or shaming a child or another adult.

- Religious abuse, such as condemning, guilting, or shaming religious beliefs.

- Abandonment abuse, such as being ignored, not listened to, or abandoned for extended periods of time.

- Disability abuse, such as being taken advantage of due to physical, intellectual, or emotional limitations.

- Borrowing/stealing money or other property and not returning it.

- Bullying, whether it takes place from child to child, adult to adult, adult to child, within a marriage, online, or in person.

Behaviors That Do Not Set True Boundaries

Not being aware of others' boundary violations is only one side of the coin. It's equally important to learn how to honor others' boundaries and how to set appropriate and respectful boundaries. Many behaviors that people may think of as setting boundaries are not boundaries at all. Here are some examples:

1. Stating Wants and Needs

One essential component of a true boundary is establishing a limit. This is a statement of what you need or want. "I need the chores to be completed as we have discussed." "I need any money borrowed to be repaid within two weeks." "I need the shouting and swearing to stop."

People often assume that when they state a limit, they have set a boundary. This isn't the case. A limit is only one component of a boundary. With no consequences or follow-through, it is essentially meaningless. When all one person does is say, "I need this from you," the other person is free to ignore the statement. There is no incentive to change the behavior.

Nor does it matter whether the limit is stated as a timid request or an angry command. "Please don't swear at me," is unlikely to change the other person's behavior. Neither is, "Don't you dare swear at me again!"

The second version might be louder and have more obvious emotion attached, but without consequences, it has no more authority than the first version.

Brad arrived for a counseling appointment feeling frustrated because he thought he had set a boundary with his wife, Jackie, when he told her she needed to throw her energy bar wrappers in the trash instead of leaving them on the counter. He told the counselor, "She won't respect any boundary I set because she doesn't listen to me."

Brad didn't realize that he had not created a boundary; he had only stated a limit.

2. Anger

When you are treated disrespectfully, a typical reaction is anger. Yet responding to the other person out of anger is not setting a boundary; it is only a way of venting and escalating feelings in a sideways manner, which can be seen as forms of bullying. This is especially true when there is a long-time pattern of disrespectful behavior. The person on the receiving end of the behavior is almost certainly going to build up a reservoir of anger and resentment. Yet the person won't know how to express the anger in a direct, clear way. Instead, if the anger eventually bursts out, it will be vented in an inappropriate fashion that is disrespectful to both parties. This "sideways" anger may come out in ways such as swearing, shouting, destroying property, malicious gossiping, and/or violence.

Anger expressed in such a way doesn't do anything to change someone's behavior in the long term. What it will do is generate more anger, which can lead to revenge. Any time your feelings are being elevated, no boundary is being set. A true boundary builds respect. An angry outburst or demand just adds more disrespect and emotional enmeshment.

When people are emotionally enmeshed, they relate to each other with sideways feelings instead of with healthy detachment and respect. Part of enmeshment is that sideways emotions drive the limits. For example, a parent might say, "If you don't clean your room, you're grounded for a month." This creates punishment rather than consequences. Later, the parent may set aside the punishment even if the room has not been cleaned because the parent has other needs or plans or is simply in a better mood. Or the child may clean the room and be punished anyway because it isn't clean enough or because the parent is angry about something else. These responses, based on the parent's emotions, are inconsistent and confusing. Both the punishments and the rewards are about the parent's feelings coming out sideways; they are not necessarily about the child at all.

In the example above, Brad told the counselor that he had asked Jackie on a number of occasions to throw the wrappers away, and she had told him she would, but she had not. Since Brad was not heard, he proceeded to escalate the situation by raising his voice with anger. This invited Jackie to respond in the same fashion, which did not help to establish a boundary.

When you have a true boundary, anger and other emotions are neutralized. True boundaries actually create a situation where feelings are not part of following through with the consequences. You are just allowing and following through with the consequences others choose with their behavior.

3. *Issuing Threats or Ultimatums*

One common element in setting boundaries successfully is reaching a point where you have had enough. You have learned enough respect for yourself that you are no longer willing to tolerate being treated disrespectfully by others. Before you can set a boundary, you need to have a clear commitment to yourself that you aren't going to accept unacceptable behavior.

It's important, though, not to confuse "having had enough" with issuing ultimatums or threats.

An ultimatum has a lot of emotion attached and is typically issued in anger. It usually starts with "if." "If you swear at me again, I'm going to leave you," is an example of an ultimatum. At first glance, it seems to state a limit and a consequence, but the consequence is actually a threat of punishment. It is too large in proportion to the offense, and there most likely is no real intention to carry it out.

Certainly, there are times when someone states an ultimatum and means it. "If you ever hit me again, I'm leaving you," might be an example of an ultimatum being given because previous attempts to set limits with a partner's abusive behavior were not taken seriously or were totally disregarded. While the historical pattern of interacting may dictate that an ultimatum is the only way for the behavior to stop, an ultimatum is not a boundary. Such an ultimatum, if given with anger in the heat of the moment, still does not effectively set a boundary. Instead, it often serves as almost a dare. It escalates the power struggle because it challenges the other person: "If you do that one more time…." In order to shore up his or her challenged power, the offender often responds by doing it one more time.

Threatening someone with a consequence you have no real power to carry out is another way of issuing a toothless ultimatum. A common way of doing this is to bring a third party into the dispute. This is both manipulative and punishing. It is a way of avoiding responsibility by making the third party your enforcer.

The classic example of avoiding responsibility is the threat, "Wait until your father comes home." This has come to be seen as almost a joke, but when it's used in real families, there is nothing funny about it. When Carlos was growing up, his alcoholic mother would get angry at him and his sister, but she would not punish them herself. Instead, when their father got home from work, she would complain to him about the kids. His response was to take both children into the bedroom and beat them with a belt. It didn't matter whether either of them had really done anything wrong; they were both punished in order to appease their mother.

When Margaret was small, her mother behaved in a similar fashion by complaining to her father when he came home. Instead of punishing Margaret, though, her father would defend her. Then her mother would get mad at him. Before long, the two of them would be arguing about something that had nothing to do with their daughter. Margaret soon learned that she could safely go to her room and play until her parents finished their argument. By then, her transgressions had been forgotten, and neither parent ever got around to punishing her.

What is common in both these examples is that the real conflict was between the parents. The anger and other emotions were being expressed sideways, with the children used as the excuse. The children were punished, or not, depending on the parents' feelings. There were no consequences for the children that had anything to do with their behavior.

It's important to clarify here that sometimes involving a third party is an appropriate part of setting a boundary. The clearest example of this is calling the police to protect yourself or someone else against violence. This is neither manipulative nor punishing. It is a way of creating safety for yourself and others, which is an integral element in setting boundaries.

Naomi's teenage grandson Tony wanted to spend the summer with his grandmother as a way to hang out with friends. Naomi created several boundaries, including a curfew. The positive consequence established for Tony respecting the curfew was that he could continue going out and visiting friends. The negative consequence was that he would choose to be home half an hour earlier the next night.

One night, with Naomi's permission, Tony went to visit his girlfriend at her father's apartment. Naomi went to pick him up at the curfew time as agreed upon, but neither Tony nor his girlfriend answered their phones. Naomi couldn't go knock on the apartment door because it was in a secured-access building. She called the police. They were able to access the apartment and get her grandson, and Naomi took Tony home. She followed through with the established consequence, and that situation did not occur again.

In this situation, Naomi had never warned or threatened to call the police if Tony did not respect his limits. Calling the police was not a punishment or an attempt to frighten or manipulate him. It was a way of creating safety for everyone in a situation where Naomi could not contact her grandson and was not sure he was all right.

When you really get to the point of having had enough, you don't need to make threats or issue ultimatums. Setting boundaries takes place a step beyond your feelings of joy, anger, fear, or hurt. It comes after you have acknowledged and processed these emotions, when you are in an emotionally neutral state of mind around the limit and the consequences you wish to establish as a boundary. You don't need to make your emotions part of the process of setting boundaries; nor is it helpful to have them involved. When the feelings are kept out of the boundary, then you don't have to say anything in the form of an ultimatum. Instead, you act by setting a clear limit and following through with consequences.

4. *Imposing Punishments and Offering Rewards*

True boundaries include both positive and negative consequences. These are not the same as punishments and rewards. The distinction may seem subtle, but it is important.

Punishments. What many people think of as consequences are actually punishments. This is especially true in interactions between parents and children. Punishments create resentments and lead the person who is first punished to respond with punishing behavior back to the person who started the pattern. With couples, the cycle of punishment-resentment-punishment may be direct and confrontational and may also be sideways. With children or others who feel they have little power in a relationship, the responding punishment may be indirect, and it will still be there. This pattern is played out with children when they ignore you, will not talk with you, or act out an unacceptable behavior.

Once you learn the differences, it's easy to tell whether a response to the violation of a limit is a punishment rather than a consequence. Here are three crucial characteristics of punishments:

The response isn't appropriate: Either it isn't related to the limit, or it's too harsh. "You didn't do the dishes, so you can't go out with your friends tomorrow night," is a punishment because it isn't related to the offense. "If you're five minutes late, you're grounded for a week," or "If I am yelled at again, I will not talk to you for a week," are punishments because they are unreasonably severe in proportion to the offense.

The response is made in anger: Suppose one Friday night, Crystal, a teenager with an 11:00 p.m. curfew, comes home at 11:30 p.m. Her mother, Diane, has spent the last half-hour worrying and imagining all sorts of horrible scenarios, and her worry erupts in anger the minute her daughter comes in the door. She immediately demands Crystal's car keys and announces that Crystal won't be allowed to drive for a week and can't leave the house for any reason other than school.

A reaction like this, in the heat of the moment and energized with emotion, is all too likely to be inappropriate to the offense. It also creates a defensive and angry response, which escalates a situation. Crystal, who hasn't even been given a chance to explain why she's late, feels attacked and gets angry in her turn. Mother and daughter end up shouting at each other.

The response creates resentment rather than respect: Most often, instead of ending the undesirable behavior, punishment actually results in more of it. Crystal, not feeling heard (regardless of whether her reason for being late is a valid one), is likely to stomp off to her room feeling unjustly treated and resentful. That resentment may well lead to her deliberately violating the curfew next time. Or, if fear of further punishment gets her to comply with the curfew, she might punish her mother in a passive-aggressive way by not speaking to her for a week. Diane, feeling that her authority has been defied, will still be angry. Nothing in the interaction has built respect or closeness between mother and daughter. This is the kind of pattern that helps create those power struggles between parents and children that are so easy to fall into and so hard to get out of.

Since children may have little or no control when they are being punished, their options of responding are typically passive/aggressive in nature. What that means is they may act out in a sideways fashion, such as not talking with the parent, or they may do something they know will upset their parent, such as pouting or breaking something.

Offering Rewards. Most often, a pattern of responding with punishments will include sometimes responding with rewards. In the example above, suppose Crystal comes home late, and her mother has just returned from a date of her own. Diane has had an enjoyable evening, which included several glasses of wine, and she is in a good mood. She waves off Crystal's explanation for being late and says, "Oh, never mind; we'll let it go this time." The same thing might happen if Diane were preoccupied with work, a television show, or a book and didn't want to take time to deal with her daughter's curfew violation. Or if she was sound asleep and didn't even realize what time her daughter came in, Crystal would be rewarded indirectly by getting away with being late.

Regardless of the specific circumstances, the common factor is that whether Crystal receives a punishment or a reward depends on Diane's mood or Diane's convenience. It has nothing directly to do with Crystal's behavior. It does nothing to teach Crystal to respect her mother's limits.

Sometimes we want to encourage positive behavior by rewarding the other person. This still limits the other person's opportunity to learn and follow the boundary in a healthy fashion. An example might be Diane letting Crystal know that if she meets her curfew for the next week, she can go to her friend's sleepover next weekend. The reward is manipulative and has an emotional string attached to the limit. Suppose Crystal meets the curfew limit for the week, yet she and her mother get into an argument on Tuesday. As a result, Diane tells Crystal she can't go to the sleepover on Friday night after all. This is an example of the emotional string associated with the reward. The reward can be lost at any time, for any reason, because of the feelings between mother and daughter.

There's one more important distinction between true boundaries with consequences and a pattern of punishments and rewards. With the latter, the person trying to set the limit is keeping control over and responsibility for what happens. Instead of having clear consequences spelled out in advance, Diane must decide each time how to respond if Crystal comes in late. If she imposes a punishment impulsively, she has to deal with the aftermath by either monitoring her daughter's compliance or modifying the punishment.

Consequences, on the other hand, kick in automatically if a limit is or is not respected. The person setting the limit has specified ahead of time exactly what will happen and takes responsibility only for his or her behavior in response. "If you do this, I will do that." The complier or violator is responsible for his or her behavior and chooses the positive or negative consequences with that behavior.

5. *Manipulation*

Manipulative behaviors are ways of expressing our feelings or wishes indirectly or in a sideways fashion. Usually, this is done to try to change someone else's behavior, to justify our own behavior, to punish, or to get even. Most commonly, people who use manipulation are not doing so deliberately or consciously. It's just that this crooked tool is the one they have learned to use. Manipulation is often learned by people who grow up in dysfunctional families where straight communication is never taught and may not even be safe.

Here are some common forms of manipulation:

Guilt: "Your mother works so hard, it just puts an extra burden on her when you don't do your chores and she has to do them." "You shouldn't miss Sunday dinner with the family because it will make your grandmother feel bad." "After all the sacrifices your father made to save money for your college education, you could at least try to get decent grades."

Revenge: "If you spend $100 on that video game for yourself, I'll spend $100 on a facial and manicure for myself."

Being a Victim or a Martyr: If Alan doesn't do the dishes on Wednesday even though it's his turn, his wife Marian might do them herself. If she does a lot of slamming cupboard doors, banging pots, grumbling, or heavy sighing, she can make sure Alan notices how hard she's working to take care of the chore he has neglected.

Silent Treatment: In the example above, Marian might either do the dishes herself or leave them undone. She would express her anger in a sideways fashion by refusing to speak to her husband for the rest of the evening.

Like punishments and threats, manipulation does nothing to create closeness or respect. It escalates feelings and conflicts rather than reducing them. In doing so, it generally creates more of the undesirable behavior.

6. Nagging

Every family seems to have one—the kid who is a night person. The kid who sleeps through the alarm or hits the snooze button twenty-seven times. The kid who, prodded by parents, finally manages to crawl out of bed just barely in time to scramble into the car, dry toast in hand, and make it to school before the last bell rings. This same drama is repeated every morning, and everyone in the family starts the day stressed and irritated because of it. No matter how much the parents scold, the child's behavior doesn't change, and they can't figure out why nagging doesn't work.

Several reasons exist for why nagging isn't effective. First of all, it's just human nature, faced with something you don't like to do, that you only do it when you have to. A child who is not a morning person will never bounce happily out of bed at 6:00 a.m. Such kids need incentives (as opposed to rewards) that are strong enough to persuade them that getting up in time for school is in their own best interest. Nagging doesn't provide that incentive.

Second, children who are being nagged, scolded, and prodded are getting attention from their parents. It's negative attention, and it's still attention.

Third, when parents are nagging, they are making themselves responsible for the child's actions. No amount of nagging will make children responsible for their own behavior. Kids can quite comfortably stay in bed until the last possible minute, knowing that Mom and Dad will make sure they don't actually miss the bus or the carpool.

Fourth, nagging creates negative energy and resentment. Nagging is just another way of making threats without any follow-through. It doesn't do anything to bring kids and parents closer together; it only leaves them feeling irritated and angry with each other.

No nagging means there will be no reminding anyone multiple times on anything. To help avoid nagging, arguing, yelling, and resentment with his kids at the start of the day, Ramon purchased each of his children their own alarm clock and indicated that, if needed, he could get them a second one as well. The boundary was that they were to get up, shower, brush teeth, brush hair, etc., eat their breakfast, pack their school bags with homework, and be in the car by 7:30 a.m. because that was the time the car would leave to ensure everyone got where they needed to go on time. If they met the limit, they experienced the positive consequence: everything went on as usual. This meant they would make it to school on time without nagging. If they did not meet the limit, they experienced the negative consequence: they would need to find their own way to school, let the school know that their tardiness was unexcused, and they would need to go to bed thirty minutes earlier that night because they obviously did not have enough time to sleep the previous night.

7. Avoidance

In many cases, going to another room or choosing not to engage with the other person for a designated amount of time are appropriate consequences for having a limit violated. "If you swear at me, I will end the conversation and leave the room for thirty minutes," is an example. This is not, however, the same as avoidance.

Avoidance is refusing to address the other person's behavior that is disrespectful and violates your boundaries. Avoidance can take a variety of forms, which often stem from anger, fear, or codependency. Storming out in anger or giving someone the silent treatment out of anger are types of avoidance. Pretending that disrespectful behavior is acceptable, because you are afraid to confront it, is also avoidance. So is allowing behavior that violates your boundaries because you are more concerned about the other person's feelings than about your own.

As another example of unhealthy avoidance, suppose a husband and wife are discussing a difficult topic, and it triggers strong feelings for one or both of them. They separate and don't talk for a day or more. When they do start talking again, they avoid the topic that triggered the sideways feelings and resentments. It's as if the previous attempt to discuss it never happened, and they don't talk about the topic until those feelings get triggered again. In contrast, it is not avoidance to create a time-out for both parties to reflect and cool down before coming back to explore the triggered feelings and continue discussing the topic.

Just to be clear, though, there are times when getting out of a dangerous situation is exactly what you may need to do for your own protection. If your partner has hit you or is threatening violence, that is not the time for confrontation. Fleeing the house under such circumstances isn't avoidance, it's taking care of yourself.

8. *Bargaining and Negotiating*

Setting a healthy true boundary is about your own behavior. It isn't a matter of negotiating a deal with the other person; it's about letting that person know how you intend to respond to their behavior. Certainly, healthy and respectful relationships include discussion, negotiating, and compromise. They aren't about one person calling the shots or setting the rules. Setting boundaries is what one person needs to do if the other person does not hold to an agreement that has been made. It isn't a negotiation, but a response to the other person's failure to respect a previous negotiation's outcome.

Jack and Samantha had been married for ten years and had what Samantha thought was a positive and healthy relationship. She trusted Jack when he told her he had to work late. This trust was lost when Samantha went out to lunch with her friend Joy, who told her she had seen Jack walking down the street arm-in-arm with another woman. After many intense discussions with Jack, Samantha decided she needed to set a boundary. She told Jack he was to limit his working late. When it was absolutely necessary, he would clearly communicate how long he would be working and also who would be working late with him. Samantha said if Jack respected this limit, she would trust him in that situation. If he did not honor the limit, her trust issue would be triggered, and in order to assure herself he could be trusted, she would need to call, show up at his work, or have someone check in on him for her. Samantha needed to set this boundary to help her feel safer and work toward reestablishing the trust she had prior to the incident.

9. Controlling Others' Behavior

Yes, the purpose of setting boundaries is to protect yourself from other people's disrespectful behavior. You do want their behavior to change. Yet you cannot make other people do or not do anything. The only behavior you have control over is your own. Boundaries are about your own behavior. "If you do this, I will do that." This does not compel others to do or not do anything. It merely sets out what your own response will be to whatever they choose to do. The person who sets the limit does not make the consequence happen, but allows it to happen. The other person's behavior is what determines whether the consequence will be positive or negative for him or her.

Many times, recipients of a boundary may feel controlled and manipulated. They typically want to blame you for "punishing them." The reality is that the boundary's recipients are attempting to control you by blaming, rather than looking at their own inappropriate behavior.

When you create true boundaries, you are not controlling others or their behavior. You are allowing them to choose either the positive or negative consequence by the behavior they choose to act out. When people initially embrace the idea of boundaries, they often approach boundary setting as a way to control or manipulate the other person. That motivation backfires because the recipient of the boundary established in this fashion will feel the manipulation and will attempt to establish some form of control in return, typically by setting counter-boundaries that cannot be enforced. When you try to create boundaries with control and manipulation, you often impose walls and punishments rather than consequences, which manifests some form of punishment in return.

Brandon and Erik had shared an apartment for several months. Erik's clutter and failure to clean up after himself was an ongoing source of tension between them. Finally, Brandon decided to set a boundary. He told Erik he would charge him $10 a day in extra rent for each day he did not pick up his mess. Erik kept on leaving stuff all over and refused to pay the $10 a day. Before long, Erik moved to a different apartment, leaving Brandon with sole responsibility for the rent and the lease.

In this case, Brandon was attempting to control Erik with a punishment rather than a consequence. He was unable to demonstrate to Erik how the $10 related to the limit, and he didn't have the ability to follow through with the consequences.

10. Struggling for Power

Setting a true boundary is not a power struggle. Instead, boundaries eliminate power struggles. This is especially true when parents set clear limits with children and consistently enforce the consequences for violating those limits. Because the kids' behavior determines the consequences, and because the consequences are applied in an emotionally neutral way, many challenges to the parents' authority simply disappear. Having true boundaries reduces the anger and other negative energy that fuels arguments and power struggles.

Donna was tired of yelling at her teenage son, Dylan, to get him to bed each night. She finally created this boundary: Dylan needed to be in bed with the lights off by 10 p.m. The positive consequence was that life would go on as usual. The negative consequence would have him in bed thirty minutes earlier the next evening. Donna was surprised by Dylan's lack of resistance when he started to conform to the boundary. She didn't have to nag or remind him to get ready for bed. His behavior changed in a positive way when he was able to see that she would consistently follow through. Every time, she followed through with the positive consequence when he complied with the boundary and the negative consequence when he did not follow the boundary. The consistency created an environment of safety for both of them, and it eliminated the previous nightly ritual of Donna yelling at Dylan to get ready for bed.

§§§§§

True boundaries create healthy patterns of respect that you may want and desire. In your relationships, you may not have experienced that respect because you have learned to follow patterns like the ones described above that promote disrespect. Changing those patterns through implementing true boundaries means you need to matter enough to yourself that you are willing to follow through with the change.

When you create clear and true boundaries, you are operating from a position of strength. You are not asking others to agree to a limit; you are setting a limit because you respect yourself. In turn, others learn to respect you and the limits you set. They also learn more respect for themselves. Because true boundaries create safety and teach respect, they build closeness and understanding.

Chapter One Reflections

To better understand true boundaries, it is helpful to reflect on who taught you boundaries and the different ways they were implemented. Who in your life has taught you how to set and follow through with true boundaries? Our first lessons on boundaries typically come from our parents or primary caregivers. If your caregivers were taught boundaries, they may have passed the boundaries on to you.

Most people grow up where there are no true boundaries; most of us were rewarded or punished based upon our caregivers' feelings at the time. This lack of structure creates much fear and uncertainty in a child's life and those feelings continue into adulthood unless some form of safety and structure is created.

If you were not raised with true boundaries or have not learned them as an adult, you may be like most people who talk about boundaries, yet do not have them. This is no fault of your own because if you were not taught true boundaries, how can you be expected to know or even understand what a true boundary is or how it can help create safety and respect in your life?

To better understand true boundaries, it is helpful to understand what they are not. If you grew up in a punishment and reward environment, you were either punished or rewarded based upon your caregiver's mood at the time. There is no safety, consistency, or respect in this type of environment. In such an environment, you learn not to matter.

When you are taught not to matter, you are also being taught that it is acceptable for others to bully, punish, manipulate, control, disrespect, and shame you. Which of these behaviors have you learned to accept in certain or all relationships?

List how boundaries were taught to you growing up.

How trusting, safe, and respected do you feel with the people in your life you feel closest with?

1 = no trust, safety, or respect   10 = complete trust, safety, or respect

Name	Trust Rating	Safety Rating	Respect Rating

Comments or reflections:

In the listed relationships that have less trust, safety, or respect than you would like, rate the areas that may be creating tension or a lack of safety.

1 = no trust, safety, or respect   10 = complete trust, safety, or respect

Name	Ignoring of Limits or Rules	Misuse of Authority	Yelling, Swearing, Threatening	Bullying	Stealing	Financial Infidelity	Physical and/ or Emotional Enmeshment

Comments or reflections:

1 = no trust, safety, respect   10 = complete trust, safety, respect

Name	Physical Abuse	Sexual Abuse	Emotional Abuse	Ritual Abuse	Religious Abuse	Abandonment Abuse	Disability Abuse

Comments or reflections:

In what relationships do you disrespect yourself?

After reviewing the assessment, in which, if any, relationships are you ready, open, and willing to create more trust, safety, or respect?

In the relationships you want to change, list the limits you have attempted to set that have not worked.

In the chart below, indicate the behaviors you have used to set the limits and rate how effective they have been for you.

1 = not effective   10 = consistently effective

Behavior	Effectiveness Rating	Comments or Reflections on Effectiveness
Anger		
Issuing Threats or Ultimatums		
Punishments or Rewards		
Walls		
Manipulation		
Guilt		
Revenge		
Victim or Martyr		
Silent Treatment		
Nagging		
Avoidance		
Bargaining and/or Negotiating		
Controlling		
Struggling for Power		

Creating True Boundaries with True Limits

"Your personal boundaries protect the inner core
of your identity and your right to choices."

— Gerard Manley Hopkins

The whole point of setting boundaries is to create a safer environment that fosters more respectful behavior. Initially, this safety and respect are for you, the person setting the boundary. For example, if you are living with someone who routinely swears and calls you names, you are not being treated with respect and your environment is not safe. As you learn more respect and appreciation for yourself and become able to set true boundaries with this person, you create a safer environment for yourself.

In the long run, true boundaries also create a safer, more respectful environment for everyone. The benefits are not just for the person creating the boundary, but for the other person as well.

While establishing true boundaries is intended to affect other people's behavior, it is not the same thing as trying to control other people's behavior. This is a very important distinction. You can't control what someone else does; people will do what they choose to do. You can only control yourself and your own behavior. By making changes in what you do, you can also, to some extent, control and change your environment and how others treat you—including the way other people behave in that environment. This happens, not because you force or manipulate them into doing anything, but because you change the way you interact with them. This shift in your behavior changes the way they interact with you. The result is an alteration of a pattern both of you have learned to follow. In this way, you can create an environment that encourages the other person to act in ways that are more respectful and allow you to feel safer. The eventual result is less conflict and more closeness in the relationship.

When Jack and Anita met, it was love at first sight. They got along well together. As the relationship developed, Jack started to show an angry side that Anita had not seen. Anita loved Jack and was able to overlook his anger because of her love. After they had gotten married and were together for about eight years, Jack's anger started to bother Anita and their relationship.

Jack and Anita had developed a pattern of Jack getting angry, Anita backing off, and then Anita resenting Jack for his anger. Jack would come back later to make up until the next explosion occurred. Anita was able to see that the pattern they had created was no longer as much about love as resentment that created distance in their relationship.

When you establish a boundary, you don't tell others what they must or must not do. Instead, you let them know what you will do in response to their behavior. You communicate clearly and specifically what the consequences will be for certain behaviors.

If the others comply with the limit you set, your response is to follow through with the positive consequences associated with the boundary. If they don't respect your limit, your response is to follow through with the negative consequences associated with the boundary. The others are still free to choose their own behavior, just as you are free to choose your response. The key to changing disrespectful behavior patterns is to follow through with the positive or negative consequences—every single time.

One of the first boundaries is recorded in Genesis 2:16-17: "The LORD God gave the man this order: You are free to eat from any of the trees of the garden except the tree of knowledge of good and evil. From that tree you shall not eat; when you eat from it you shall die."

In this example, Adam and Eve were given a limit, a positive and negative consequence that directly related to the limit, and follow through. The limit was to not eat from the tree of knowledge. The positive consequence was being able to remain in the Garden of Eden. The negative consequence was them choosing to leave the Garden of Eden and experience death with their action of eating the forbidden fruit. God gave them a choice that would be played out with their actions.

Before we get into the process of creating boundaries, it's important to clarify some terms. First of all, it's worth reiterating that true boundaries include three components: setting a limit, establishing positive consequences for respecting the limit and negative consequences for violating it, and following through with those consequences. The term "boundary," as used throughout this book, includes all three parts of the larger process. It is not interchangeable with "limit," which describes the specific behavior you need or want from the other person.

Second, boundaries are intended to create safety in your environment and respect in your relationships. When I say this to clients, sometimes I get the response, "Well, my environment is safe, so why do I have to change anything?" Yet often, the situation they have described to me includes arguing, yelling, being ignored, or other forms of disrespect or even emotional abuse. They just have never thought of this as unsafe.

When people think of safety in terms of boundaries, they may associate it with truly abusive or life-threatening circumstances where someone is being threatened, bullied, or hit. Many of the examples in this and later chapters deal with much less serious scenarios. Using the term "safety" to describe some of these situations may seem exaggerated or extreme. Yet an environment that fosters chaos, resentment, tension, arguments, and anger even in relatively small ways is certainly not a safe or respectful space to share with the people we love. It creates distance instead of closeness. Emotional safety and comfort are as essential in healthy relationships as physical safety, and in many cases, that safety and comfort are threatened by even minor patterns of disrespect. Tolerating disrespect in any form from others in our day-to-day interactions violates our emotional safety and is a way of being disrespectful to ourselves.

The process of creating a boundary includes defining an appropriate limit, establishing positive and negative consequences, communicating the limit and consequences (preferably in writing) to the other person, and following through consistently with the consequences. Each boundary needs to be tailored to a given relationship and situation. The process of creating a boundary remains the same, but this is not a cookie-cutter approach. The limits and consequences appropriate in a particular case depend on many factors: people's personalities, the individual histories that shape their "hot buttons" and issues, their relationship history, the closeness of their relationship, the issues of contention between them, and all the other elements that make their situation unique.

What is a large boundary to one person may be small to another. What is an appropriate consequence in one situation may be a punishment in another. The examples in this chapter and throughout this book are meant to help you understand what boundaries are and how to create them. However, they are meant as suggestions, not scripts. They offer possibilities to help you get started. Feel free to practice with them and use them as learning tools, and please keep in mind that you'll want to modify them to fit your own needs and circumstances.

Writing Out Boundaries

When establishing boundaries, it is helpful and important to write them out so they can be referred to and/or modified as situations change. The benefits of writing out boundaries include:

- **Providing a document to refer back to when the boundary is being challenged.** When boundaries are first being established, they will be challenged. One way people challenge boundaries is to say "You never told me that." If the boundary is already written out, there is no need to argue; you can just remind them to look at the boundaries.

- **Creating a space to more objectively create the boundaries, which takes more emotion out of the process.** When you write a boundary in the heat of the moment, often it is written in anger without emotional objectivity. The added time creates space for more objective reflecting on the situation and boundary.

- **Additional time for reflection, which allows changes to occur before the boundaries are presented.** Many times, the first draft of a boundary is not the final version because there may be some emotional issues that limit objectivity. The initial written boundary may be difficult to follow through with or may be impractical.

Example: Jackie wanted to establish a boundary with Bob around his chewing tobacco. Jackie did not like his chewing because of the smell when they would kiss and her fear for his health. In the heat of an argument over chewing, Jackie indicated that she was going to throw all of his cans of chew away to get him to stop.

This was not a boundary because there were no positive and negative consequences, just a punishment with control. This was shared in the heat of an argument, so the framework was established in anger rather than objectivity. Finally, following through with throwing all the cans of chew away will not stop Bob from chewing because he will just buy more and learn to hide them better from Jackie.

- **Time to reflect on how the positive and negative consequences directly relate to the limit.** This additional time is also helpful to reflect on how the consequences directly relate to the limit and the likelihood that the consequences can be consistently followed through. This time is critical because when the boundary is first established, the person you are setting the boundary with may reframe the negative consequence as a punishment unless adequate time to think through the issues is properly given.

Example: Erika's parents, Greg and Joyce, would not allow her to use any of her screens, including watching TV, until her homework was completed. Erika felt her parents wanted to punish her because of the way they first presented this boundary. With some reflecting and coaching, Greg and Joyce wrote a boundary that shifted the responsibility from them to Erika.

Erika was to get her homework completed prior to using any

screens and TV. As soon as she completed her homework, she was free to use the screens and TV as usual. If Erika chose not to complete her homework at school when she had time or chose to do something other than her homework when she got home, she was also choosing not to use her screens or TV.

While that may seem like a small change with a similar outcome, when Erika realized it was her choice not to use the screens or TV, it helped her make better choices for completing her homework.

When boundaries are written out, it is important to have an additional boundary clause. Human beings can be amazingly legalistic thinkers; we are very good at finding and slipping through the tiniest of loopholes. So I always include a final statement like, "Other boundaries may be implemented and will be established as necessary to help everyone in the house/relationship feel respected and loved."

Setting a Limit

When asked, most people believe they have boundaries. Further inquiry shows that the person may have established a limit but not a boundary. In the boundary-setting process, the limit is the first of the three steps that create the boundary. The limit by itself is not a boundary.

The limit is what the person setting the boundary needs or wants in order to create more safety and respect in a relationship. Suppose, for example, Lonnie is frustrated with the lack of respect from his teenage children, Mark and Selena, over doing the dishes. He's sick of seeing dirty dishes in the sink and having arguments over whose turn it is to do them. He has tried nagging, scolding, punishments, and bribes, but nothing has worked. Half the time, he ends up doing the dishes himself because one of the kids "forgot"—again. He's feeling angry and frustrated, and so are his kids.

Finally, Lonnie has had enough. He is ready to establish a boundary around doing the dishes. He is willing to do what it takes to create a safer, more respectful way of dealing with this issue. How does he go about it?

The first step in creating a true boundary is to establish an appropriate limit. This is not as simple as it might seem. It's a good idea to think it through carefully rather than setting a limit impulsively. It is helpful to ask these questions: Where am I not feeling safe or respected? What respectful limit might I set that would change the situation? If I were treating myself with respect, what behavior would I want from the other person?

If someone asked Lonnie what he wanted as a limit, his first response would probably be, "For the kids to do the dishes without all this arguing." However, he's already been telling them this is what he wants, and it hasn't worked.

What Lonnie really wants is a system that provides fairness (he, Mark, and Selena all take turns doing dishes), builds respect (gets rid of the arguments and power struggles around doing dishes), and increases family closeness (he and the kids can spend evenings together pleasantly instead of fighting about doing dishes). To achieve this, a limit needs to be fair rather than punishing, clear and specific, and appropriate to the issue at hand.

Being specific with a limit is essential. Not "I need you to be nicer to me," but "I need to be spoken to in a respectful tone instead of yelling." Not "I need you to do your share of housework," but "I need you to clean the upstairs bathroom every weekend and take turns with me vacuuming once a week."

Another aspect of setting a limit is that it's unilateral. You don't ask the other person's permission to set the limit. You don't negotiate the limit with that person. You decide what you need to feel safe and respected, and you communicate that limit to the other person. The limit is being established because you need safety and respect that you are not receiving. It is not a bargain or a negotiated agreement.

As the parent, Lonnie certainly does not need his children's approval or agreement before he sets a limit about household chores. Even if he were setting a limit with his spouse or another adult, however, he would not need that person's okay. The boundary creator does not need the other person's agreement to or approval of the limit to set it. In fact, most commonly a boundary is set because the other person has either refused to agree to a limit, or has agreed to one but has not respected it.

After some consideration, Lonnie comes up with the following limit: "Mark will do the dishes on Monday and Wednesday. Selena will do them on Tuesday and Thursday. Lonnie will do them on Friday, Saturday, and Sunday. Doing the dishes includes putting away the clean dishes in the dishwasher; clearing off the table and putting leftovers in the fridge; rinsing today's dirty dishes and loading them in the dishwasher; hand-washing anything that can't go in the dishwasher; wiping off the table, counters, and stove; and running the dishwasher. The dishes need to be done prior to getting ready for bed."

Lonnie puts this limit in writing. It's clear, specific, and fair. He has the first component of a boundary, and he isn't finished yet.

Sometimes, when you are being treated with disrespect, others will want to give advice like, "You need to tell them to stop doing that." If setting boundaries were that simple, we would all be much better at it than we are. Yes, communicating to the other person exactly what limit you want and need is part of the process of creating a boundary. But merely telling someone to stop acting in a disrespectful manner isn't enough. Setting a limit by itself is merely information. You may be clear and specific about what you need; you may write it down and even get the other person to agree to it—but that does not establish a boundary that will change the behavior.

Most people are not willing to change what they are doing until they are given a reason to change. You telling them to stop a given behavior doesn't provide that reason. Giving people a reason to change what they are doing is the purpose of the second component of a true boundary: consequences. Consequences will be the subject of our next chapter.

§§§§§

Limits give guidance and direction around areas of disrespect in a relationship, yet limits alone are not true boundaries. Time, reflection, and writing out limits can be the foundation of creating true boundaries.

Chapter Two Reflections

Most people think that creating limits is a boundary. The limit is the first step and is an important piece of a boundary. Because of limits' importance in establishing a true boundary, it is essential that sufficient time is allowed to formulate the limit.

Limits are established when there is a lack of trust, safety, or respect. When we attempt to control these aspects of a relationship, they get challenged to the point that there is even less trust, safety, or respect. When you realize you can only control yourself, the opportunity to create true boundaries can occur.

Establishing true boundaries can be difficult at first because it requires responding differently to a situation than before. As you create success with one boundary with the person, you can add additional boundaries to build more confidence in establishing the difficult boundaries. This all starts with successful reflection during the limit-writing process.

Are there areas of your relationships you have attempted to control without success? If the answer is yes, fill in the chart below listing the relationships and the areas in which you would like to create positive changes.

Name	Areas of Relationship You Wish to Change

Now in the next chart, list all the limits you would like to set with each person. Make sure they are specific limits with which you can follow through.

Name	Limit

Establishing True Consequences

> "In nature there are neither rewards nor punishments;
> there are consequences."
>
> — Robert Green Ingersoll

Consequences are what will happen if the limit is respected and what will happen if it is not. A boundary always needs to include positive consequences for respecting the limit and negative ones for violating it.

A consequence may be a specific action on the part of the boundary setter. Here is an example: "I need the name calling and swearing to stop. When the swearing and name calling is not present, we are free to connect and communicate respectfully. If I am being called names or being sworn at, I will leave the room, and we will come back to the conversation in half an hour, at which time I expect apologies for the disrespect, one for me and another for you. If the apologies are not given, I will limit any form of communication until the apologies are sincerely given."

Sometimes, though, both negative and positive consequences are natural outcomes of the other person's actions. An example might be: "If you do your laundry, you will have clean clothes to wear. If you don't do your laundry, you won't have any clean clothes."

In creating a boundary with his children around doing the dishes, Lonnie established the following consequences:

Positive: "If you do the dishes on your assigned night, life goes on as usual." As much as possible, it is better to make consequences short and to the point because doing so helps create clarity and neutralize the emotions.

Negative: "If you don't do the dishes on your assigned night, you will do them, plus the following day's dishes, on the next night. This means you will take the next person's turn and they will get a night off. You will also do the dishes the third night if it is your usual turn. If you don't do the dishes on the second night, you will do dishes for all three days on the third night, even if that night is not your usual turn. Also, since there seems to be a lack of time to do the dishes, starting the second day, you are choosing not to use your cell phone, computer, and TV until the dishes are done so these distractions don't take time away from doing the dishes."

Lonnie puts the limit and consequences in writing, reviews them with the kids, gives Selena and Mark each a copy, and posts a copy in the kitchen.

Appropriate Consequences

Establishing consequences, even more than defining limits, requires careful thought. Both positive and negative consequences need to be appropriate, specific, and clearly communicated. When you set consequences impulsively, in anger, or as part of an argument, they are likely to be punishments or attempts to get revenge. Punishment always has some form of punishment returned, so if you give punishment to someone, you can always expect some form of punishment in return. To help decide whether a given consequence you are considering, especially a negative consequence, is appropriate, I suggest asking yourself the following questions:

1. **Is the consequence on the same scale or level of severity as the respectful/disrespectful behavior?** An appropriate positive consequence often may be that no change of behavior is necessary, meaning life goes on as usual. An appropriate negative consequence for neglecting to walk the dog, for example, might be taking a sibling's turn to walk the dog for the next day. An inappropriate consequence, or punishment, might be getting rid of the dog.

2. **Is the consequence directly related to the behavior?** An appropriate positive consequence for teenagers who come home on time for their curfew is having the same curfew time the next evening. An appropriate negative consequence for a teenager who comes home late might be needing to come home earlier the next night, perhaps thirty minutes earlier. An inappropriate negative consequence might be having a cell phone taken away for a week. When you establish a consequence, you need to be prepared to explain to the recipient how that consequence relates to the limit. Thinking through that explanation ahead of time will help you clarify for yourself that the consequence is an appropriate one.

3. **Is the consequence clear and specific?** An appropriate positive consequence for arriving for dinner at the set time is the opportunity to eat dinner and connect with the family. An appropriate negative consequence for violating a limit of "I need you to call and let me know if you're going to be home late for dinner" might be, "If you don't call, you are choosing to eat dinner by yourself, and

you'll need to reheat or prepare your own dinner when you get home." An inappropriate consequence might be, "If you don't call, you'll be sorry when you get home."

4. **Is the consequence something you can and will follow through with?** Consequences need to be either natural outcomes of the other person's behavior ("If you don't do your laundry, you won't have any clean clothes") or be within the control of the person setting the limit. It makes no sense, for example, for a parent to set a consequence for a teenage driver of, "If you drive faster than the speed limit, you'll get a ticket." The parent has no power to issue traffic tickets. The parent could, however, require that any speeding tickets be paid from the child's own funds.

Another consequence within the parent's control might be having the child give the parents the car keys so that time can be given to reflect on the reason for speeding and have that reason shared. The keys could be returned after the child has written an explanation for why they were speeding in the first place. This provides an opportunity for the child to reflect and learn, which could help build safer driving habits.

Consequences chosen in anger or without careful thought often turn out to be ineffective for two reasons. First, when anger is involved, the response will be a punishment rather than a consequence. Second, many times the boundary setter isn't willing to or doesn't have the ability to consistently follow through with the consequences. Ironically, such careless consequences can even be more of a punishment for the person setting them than they are for the recipient.

To illustrate, let's go back for a moment to the example from Chapter One of Diane and her daughter Crystal. When Crystal comes home past her curfew, suppose Diane takes her car keys and says Crystal won't be allowed to drive for a week and can't leave the house for any reason other than school. When she issues this angry response, Diane isn't remembering that Crystal has an after-school job three days a week. Being unable to drive or leave the house except for school means Crystal can't go to work. That leaves Diane in an uncomfortable position. She will either have to modify the punishment to let Crystal drive to work, leave her own job to take her daughter to work, or insist that Crystal miss three days of work. Backing down on the punishment will probably leave Diane feeling as if she has "lost" and her daughter has "won." Inconveniencing herself to enforce the punishment will most likely make Diane angry and resentful. Allowing Crystal to miss work will have its own consequences, leaving Crystal angry and feeling unfairly treated. Diane has stated a consequence that isn't realistic to follow through with, and the result is increased resentment on both sides and more distance between mother and daughter.

5. **Is the consequence likely to reduce resentment and conflict or increase them?** Remember, a boundary is intended to foster respect and closeness. In the short term, it may create more anger on the part of the recipient, and in the long term, it will reduce anger and conflict. If a consequence is likely to create more anger rather than less for the boundary setter, it is probably a punishment. A consequence needs to be strong enough to get the other person's attention and create some discomfort, but not harsh enough to be punitive. Even when a consequence is otherwise appropriate, it can be a punishment if it has emotional strings attached. An example of an emotional string is a "gotcha" feeling on the part of the person setting the boundary.

Jack had had enough of Betty's drinking. He decided to set a boundary that as long as Betty did not drink, life would go on as usual and they could freely connect with each other. If Jack learned Betty was drinking, he would stop connecting with her until she was sober and apologized.

One evening, they went out to dinner with friends. Jack decided he would have a beer. When Betty realized Jack was drinking, she also ordered a beer. With enthusiasm, Jack immediately let her know she had broken the boundary. Jack's response indicated that this was not a true boundary; rather, it was a "gotcha," setting Betty up to fail.

The goal is not to punish, but to take sideways feelings out of the interactions and create an environment for reflection that ultimately will heal difficulties in the relationship, build respect, and bring people closer.

6. **Does this consequence address the right problem?** Frank and Kasey have been married for fifteen years. They consistently argue about money. Frank is a spender and Kasey is a saver. Since Frank spent money allocated for a much-needed new car, Kasey decided she wanted to create a boundary around money with Frank.

Kasey set a limit that any money in the joint account was to be discussed and approved together prior to being used for any purchase. The positive consequence would be improved communication around money issues and less arguing because both would be involved in the decision.

Kasey had the negative consequence of placing her whole paycheck into her personal account rather than into the joint account until the amount that was not approved was replaced by Frank. This made money unavailable for Frank to use. Kasey made significantly more money than Frank and was prepared to ensure all the mutual bills were appropriately paid from her private account.

While allocating less money into the joint account allowed Kasey to create more control with the money, it actually created more anger and resentment from Frank.

Most spending problems are associated with patterns of codependency and/or self-worth. The boundary did create more resentment because Frank's spending patterns were associated with his lack of self-worth, which was his way of hiding his emotional insecurities around Kasey making more money than him.

7. **Is there room to ramp up the consequence?** It's best to start with the mildest consequences appropriate to the limit. That way, if someone continues to violate the limit, you can escalate the consequences until you find one that creates enough discomfort to give the other person a reason to comply. You can't do this if you start out with too severe of a consequence. You can always ramp up consequences if you need to, but it's hard to ramp them down.

As an example, suppose Kendrick has started skipping school. The first level of negative consequences might be: "I won't excuse your absences." If the unexcused absence is not enough of a consequence to motivate change, an additional negative consequence might be, "Kendrick will be choosing to write a sincere apology letter about his actions to each teacher as well as himself for the disrespect shown to these people. To ensure there is time for proper reflection, Kendrick is choosing with his behavior to use no electronic devices until the apologies are written." The next step may be to involve the principal and a counselor. After that might come involving the police or the court system. Typically, the first or second consequence will be enough to motivate a positive response. Again, in a situation like this, it's essential to explore the problem thoroughly, since skipping school is often a symptom of deeper difficulties.

Life Goes On as Usual

While many of the above questions have a greater focus on choosing negative consequences, it's equally important to define appropriate positive consequences. In general, these can be summed up as some variation on, "Life goes on as usual."

People have questioned how "Life goes on as usual" can be a positive consequence. For one thing, life "as usual" may not be particularly comfortable around the issue in question. If it were, there would probably not be a need to create a boundary in the first place. Second, life going on as usual doesn't immediately appear to be a positive consequence because it seems to be the same thing that would happen if no boundary were created.

There are several reasons why "Life goes on as usual" is indeed a positive consequence:

- Even if the usual pattern is uncomfortable, keeping it may feel like a positive outcome to boundary recipients because it allows them to stay in what is familiar.

- Typically, what is "usual" will gradually change for the better as the boundary creates more safety in a relationship.

- Perhaps most important, when the boundary setter follows through, neutrally and unemotionally, with positive and negative consequences, that, in itself, changes the behavior pattern in a relationship. The tension between the boundary setter and the recipient is eased to at least some degree by the neutrality of the follow-through. In practice, then, "Life goes on as usual" often plays out as "Life goes on with less conflict and tension."

Many times, there's no need to state anything more than this as the positive consequence. In other cases, it might be appropriate to include a more specific statement. Here are just a couple of examples:

- "If you are ready to leave for school by 7:30, we will have time to pick up your friend Jamie."

- "If you call to let me know you'll be late, with a respectful reason, I'll wait for you so we can eat dinner together."

One caveat exists when it comes to being specific with positive consequences: you want to be careful that they are actually consequences and not rewards. Many times, the person setting the boundary believes it's necessary to offer some type of reward as a positive consequence. Rewards create a level of expectation that most likely cannot be maintained in the long run. Rewards add feelings to the interaction, while with a true boundary, the feelings are neutral.

Stating a positive consequence as, "Life goes on as usual," is similar to choosing the smallest appropriate negative consequence. Both of these tend to neutralize emotions and conflict. Stating a more specific positive consequence, however, can sometimes be manipulative, a way of nudging the other person toward complying with your limit by praising or rewarding them. It can also be unsustainable on a practical level. For example, a reward such as, "If you finish cleaning your room, I'll take you to the park to play," might not always be possible or realistic to carry out. When you offer praise or rewards, you are still trying to control others' behavior instead of giving them the freedom and responsibility to choose and allowing both the positive and negative consequences to speak for themselves.

Written Apologies

An often appropriate negative consequence is a sincere formal written apology to everyone being offended, including having the person violating the boundary write it to themselves. A verbal apology is often less useful because it can easily be provided with little thought or sincerity. Requiring the apology in writing is preferable for several reasons: it takes effort and thought, it has to be uniquely done, the recipient can tell if it's not sincere, and it encourages reflection. Writing an apology gives people an opportunity to think about the disrespect in their behavior. A written apology is not a punishment, yet it's just uncomfortable enough that someone won't want to do it every day.

Having the boundary violator write a formal written apology to themselves tends to create the most tension and is actually the most important apology because it creates a deeper level of reflection for the violator. It also creates a greater chance that the boundary will be maintained. The formal written apology from the violator to the violator actually helps create a greater likelihood of positive change.

Anita established a boundary with her friend Kari around being yelled at. Anita indicated that as long as she was not yelled at, life would go on as usual. If Kari decided to yell at Anita, Anita would limit their interactions to only what was necessary until Anita received a sincere formal written apology and heard Kari read it to her. Kari would also write a sincere formal apology to herself and read it to Anita.

The first time Kari violated this boundary, Anita received a sincere formal written apology from Kari the next day. Anita continued to limit her interactions because Kari refused to write a sincere formal apology to herself. When Kari finally wrote and shared the apology, they reconnected as usual.

Later, Kari shared with Anita that the apology to Anita was much easier to write than the one to herself. Kari proceeded to share how, in the apology to herself, she was able to see different ways she had hurt and disrespected herself, and that this helped her become more aware of her behavior. Kari indicated that the new awareness impacted her need to yell at Anita, and the pattern slowly shifted away from yelling and toward more positive interactions.

The bottom line in creating boundaries is that the goal is not merely for the other person to comply with your limit. It is also to build a pattern of mutual respect that provides safety and increased closeness in the relationship. The most appropriate and effective consequences are those that give the other person a choice as well as enough discomfort when the boundary is violated to encourage reflection, and not enough discomfort to foster resentment.

Help from a Neutral Third Party

Especially when you are learning to create true boundaries, it can be very helpful to discuss possible limits and consequences with a neutral third party. Someone who isn't directly involved can help you clarify your thinking, process your emotions, and get past your own perceptions. It's important to choose this person wisely. He or she should not be a family member who will likely have the same perspective you do, or someone else who is emotionally connected to the situation. The temptation is to find someone who will reinforce your emotions and pair with you, but this isn't going to help. At the same time, you don't want someone who will pair with the other person. You might choose a counselor, a pastor, a Twelve-Step sponsor, or someone in a recovery support group. What's most important is that this person be trustworthy, aware of true boundaries, and able to give you neutral and honest feedback.

In especially difficult or emotionally charged situations, like setting boundaries with an abusive spouse, I would recommend working with a counselor who can be emotionally neutral and objective. In addition to having the counselor help you define appropriate limits and consequences, it could also be valuable to involve him or her when you present the boundary to your partner. The counselor's role is not to enforce the consequences, but to support you and facilitate what initially is likely to be a difficult conversation.

Communicating the Limit

Just as with setting the limit, the boundary setter doesn't need to get the other person's approval or buy-in to establish the consequences. It is important, though, to give that person advance notice of the limit and the consequences. Sometimes people think advance notice means they have to give people "one more chance" to comply with the limit before they create the boundary. To be fair, they think they need to say, "If you do that again…." Giving a warning like this is not necessary. In fact, it usually comes across as issuing a threat or an ultimatum, which tends to increase conflict rather than decreasing it the way a true boundary does. Using "If you do that again" is an indication that no boundary exists because it demonstrates inconsistent follow-through.

All the advance notice others need is clear communication of the limit and the consequences, shared clearly only the one time prior to the boundary enforcement. I strongly recommend putting this in writing so everyone involved has a clear understanding of the limit, the positive consequences, and the negative consequences. This gives boundary recipients a chance to read the document and maybe even sign off on it. Reading the document is not for the purpose of discussing or negotiating it. Signing it is not meant to imply they agree with the limit or make a commitment to comply with it; it is just to acknowledge that they have read it.

It's a good idea to provide a copy of the boundary document for each person or maybe to post it in a place where everyone will notice it. This makes it harder for the boundary recipient to claim, "I didn't understand," or "You never said that." Part of the power of true boundaries comes just from the clear statement and communication. It provides accountability and consistency because everyone can see what's written down. That same accountability makes it easier for the boundary setter to follow through with the consequences.

Triggering Issues

Presenting the written boundary is best done at a neutral time and not in the middle of an argument. For example, couples often argue when an issue that comes up triggers an emotional response in one of them. Carrie was upset because Herb was an hour late getting home and did not notify her that he would be late. In the midst of her fear and anger, she decided to let Herb know that the next time he was late without prior notice, he would have to sleep on the couch. Since feelings were heightened with both Carrie and Herb, bringing up the boundary at this time turned into an argument, which took the focus off the boundary. If Carrie had been able to take time to reflect and write out the boundary, the boundary could have been more neutral and objective. Presenting it to Herb at a time when both spouses were calm would make it more likely to be heard and respected because he could be in a better position to actually listen rather than defend himself.

When one person is triggered is not the time to try to have a conversation. The emotion flooding the brain can literally make it impossible for someone to understand or even hear what the other person is saying. When someone's emotions are triggered in this way, what is needed is a time-out to deal with and reflect on the emotion. For this reason, a consequence of, "If I am yelled at, the conversation is over," is often not particularly useful. Many times, one partner will appreciate the conversation being over so they don't have to look at the issue until it comes up again in another argument. A more appropriate consequence might be, "If I am yelled at, we'll take a time-out for fifteen minutes and then come back to the conversation expecting to explore the feelings in a way that resolves the conflict on that issue."

The purpose of the time-out is not to wait until the anger or other triggered emotion is gone. If you and your partner wait that long, chances are you won't get back to the issue because you will no longer feel the need to work through it. The issue has been stored away for the time being so you can avoid it, and it has not been resolved. It's still there, waiting to be triggered the next time. Instead, the time-out is to allow the emotions to subside enough so both of you can identify and reflect on them. Then, when the two of you get back to the discussion, the triggered emotions have cooled enough so you can begin to talk constructively about the feelings creating the disrespect and work through the issue.

If a triggering issue is a large one or a well-established pattern of abusive behavior exists, it's often necessary to have an even longer time-out, which should be no more than twenty-four hours. In such a situation, an appropriate consequence might be, "If I am yelled at, we won't communicate until I receive sincere written apologies to me from you and from you to you on this issue."

With issues that trigger strong emotion, it's especially important to fine-tune the boundary to respect each other's true emotional needs. The limit and consequences need to be tied to the issue and the situation in a way that will help the person triggered to want to reconnect and move forward.

Once appropriate limits and consequences have been set, then comes the next crucial step in the process of creating a boundary. This step is following through, consistently and calmly, with the consequences. The follow-through will be the subject of Chapter Four.

Chapter Three Reflections

True boundaries cannot exist without appropriate consequences that directly relate to the limit being established. The consequences cannot be larger or smaller than the situation demands. It is important to be able to share how the consequence directly relates to the limit.

If the limit is seen as a wall, punishment, or reward, it is about your feelings driving the process and true consequences are not in place. Appropriate time to reflect on the consequences is important to allow them to be emotionally neutral and respectful.

When presenting the boundary and limits, it is important to let the other person know you are following through with the consequence they are choosing with their behavior. Many times, parents have shared that they are taking away screens because of homework or grades. I invite them to reframe the consequences to let the child know that they are not taking the screens away from them; rather, the child is choosing not to use the screens because they are choosing not to complete their homework or maintain a certain grade.

From the relationships mentioned in Chapter Two in which you would like to create positive change, list the person's name, the limits you want to establish, a positive consequence that directly relates to the situation, and a negative consequence that directly relates to the situation. This creates the foundation for a boundary.

Name	Limit You Wish To Establish	Positive Consequence	Negative Consequence

Comments or reflections:

What feelings did you have as you wrote about the consequences above?

_____

_____

_____

Which feelings will hinder your ability to follow through with the consequences?

_____

_____

_____

Will the written consequences increase or decrease resentment or conflict?

_____

_____

_____

Do the consequences address the issue the limit is establishing?

_____

_____

_____

Explain the process of ramping up the established negative consequences if needed.

_____

_____

_____

Explain how positive consequences are closely related to "life going on as usual."

_____

_____

_____

To better understand the process of a sincere formal written apology, write a sincere formal apology to yourself in relation to one of these limits you wish to establish and how you have disrespected yourself in the past by not having this boundary.

Find a neutral third party to walk through each of the limits and consequences you wish to establish to verify their emotional neutrality.

Reflect on when and how you will present these boundaries to the person you wish to establish a boundary with.

CREATING SAFETY WITH CONSISTENT FOLLOW-THROUGH

"You must know in your heart before anyone else does
what is going to be good and then follow through."

— Bill Budge

Follow-through is the essential part of the process, the "cooking," if you will, that takes limits and consequences and turns them into true boundaries. Your role as the boundary setter is to ensure that the consequences take place—every single time. Either you take the actions you have said you will take, or you stay out of the way and allow natural consequences to happen.

Consistency in following through is what makes boundaries effective. Lack of follow-through, more than anything else, is what causes the breakdown of boundaries. Sometimes people use the terms "weak" or "strong" to describe boundaries. What they mean by these terms is how consistently the boundary setter follows through with consequences. They assume that if you follow through consistently, it's a strong boundary, and if you don't, it's a weak one. This is not an accurate way to look at boundaries. What really happens is that if you fail to follow through one time out of 100, you don't have a boundary. You can follow through ninety-nine times in a row, then make an exception the one hundredth time, "just this once"—and the boundary is gone and must be reestablished.

Instead of thinking in terms of whether boundaries are weak or strong, it's more effective to remember Yoda's advice from *The Empire Strikes Back*: "Do. Or do not. There is no try." Either you follow through every single time and the boundary is there, or you don't follow through and the boundary no longer exists.

Characteristics of Effective Boundaries

While consistency is the most vital part of following through, several other factors matter as well. In order for boundaries to be effective, they need these characteristics:

- They are emotionally neutral.
- They withstand being tested by the boundary recipient.
- They allow the recipient to choose the consequences.
- They divide responsibility appropriately between the boundary setter and the boundary recipient.

Let's look at each of these characteristics in more detail.

1.   Emotional Neutrality

When you react to disrespectful behavior with emotions such as anger and hurt, you often end up imposing punishments even when you think you're responding with consequences. This type of reaction can create more anger on the part of the other person. The anger feels punishing, which creates a punishing response. What happens is that both of you get stuck in an escalating pattern of disrespectful behavior, angry response, resentment, more disrespectful behavior, and more anger.

Consequences, by contrast, are emotionally neutral. They are established in an emotionally "lukewarm" environment, when you have a chance to think them through and define them logically. Becoming able to act with this kind of emotional detachment and neutrality, for many of us, means learning to resolve our difficult emotions. Since this is a subject in itself, this section will only focus on the "what" of emotional neutrality, leaving the "how" for a fuller explanation in Chapter Six.

When you define limits and establish consequences at a neutral time, instead of in the middle of an argument or out of anger at the other person's lack of respect, those limits and consequences are much more likely to be appropriate. As a result, your boundaries are much more likely to be effective. This is another reason for placing boundaries in writing. The process of writing them down not only helps you create clear and appropriate limits and consequences, but also helps reduce your emotional involvement. The written boundary document becomes almost like a policies and procedures manual for a company: it presents things in a neutral way and provides guidelines so everyone knows what to expect.

The emotional neutrality of true boundaries is similar to what Twelve-Step programs describe as "detachment with love." When someone violates a limit, the boundary setter chooses not to take the action personally. Following through with consequences is not done in a punitive way. It does not vary depending on someone's emotional state at the time a limit is violated; it avoids the punishment/reward pattern of "If I'm in a bad mood, I might punish you; if I'm in a good mood, I might not." Because the consequences are clearly specified ahead of time, following through with them is not personal or emotionally charged. The boundary setter might feel some sadness or hurt if the other person doesn't respect a limit, and yet the deep emotions do not get triggered or escalated.

Appropriate consequences foster emotional neutrality and do not support holding grudges. A grudge is just another word for resentment. If when you establish a consequence, you feel any sense of mean satisfaction, vindictiveness, or vengefulness, your response is likely too harsh, a punishment rather than a consequence. A true boundary allows and encourages others to reflect on their own behavior instead of punishing them.

An important component of emotional neutrality is allowing the consequences to speak for themselves. There's no need to say anything if limits are violated—the consequences do the talking for you. This also applies when limits are respected. Praising someone for their compliance means that you, as the boundary setter, are still trying to control the situation instead of allowing the other person to freely choose whether to comply.

2.   Testing

One of the biggest challenges to emotional neutrality comes when the other person tests the boundaries. It helps to keep in mind that boundary testing is a natural and even essential part of creating a boundary. The only way for the recipient to know whether you have a real boundary is to test it.

When you begin setting boundaries, you are changing your part of an existing pattern of disrespectful behavior both parties are accustomed to. Both of you have learned this pattern together, and it is familiar. When you do something to break that pattern, then it's perfectly natural for others to object and to challenge the limits you set. They will want to hold on to the old familiar pattern. This is normal. It is to be expected. This does not mean they hate you, are intentionally being difficult, will never change, or are bad people. It is just a natural response to a change that is unfamiliar and uncomfortable.

Testing a boundary also means the recipient is making sure you can be trusted to say what you mean and mean what you say. It's the recipient's job to challenge your boundaries, which is not necessarily the same thing as the recipient wanting the boundaries to fail. When I worked with teenagers in the legal system, some of them told me directly that they wished their parents would set boundaries with them. They needed and wanted to know what the limits were because it created a level of safety, security, and a feeling of mattering and being loved. Without those limits, their boundary-testing behavior became more and more extreme until they ended up in the juvenile justice system.

When people test your boundaries, they are also verifying that they matter to you. This is especially true with parents and children. When a parent doesn't follow through with boundaries, the message communicated to the kids is, "You don't matter enough for me to make the effort to set limits and follow through with consequences." When parents do follow through, the message they communicate is, "You are important to me, and I want to teach you to respect others and yourself."

Because so few of us are taught about true boundaries, many families develop patterns of unclear expectations, unspoken rules, and inconsistent punishments and rewards. Such patterns foster miscommunication, mistrust, and disrespect. Boundaries, on the other hand, clarify and communicate limits and expectations. This is just one more reason it's helpful to write out and post boundaries so everyone knows exactly what they are. Such clear communication and consistent follow-through build trust, which fosters respect. The two go together. If I can't trust you, I won't respect you; and if you don't respect yourself, I won't trust or respect you.

Having the recipient test your boundaries, then, while it can be challenging and frustrating, is an important part of the process. Here are just a few of the ways people might test boundaries:

- Getting angry

- Accusing you of being manipulative

- Blaming

- Trying to make you feel guilty

- Wheedling and making promises to respect your limit if you don't follow through with consequences

- Making threats

- Finding loopholes

- Setting counter-boundaries

This last one, counter-boundaries, needs a little explanation. Sometimes you might create a boundary and the other person says, "Well, then, I'll do the same thing. The same limits and consequences apply to you." If it's a true boundary, you won't have a problem with that. You won't want or need to act in the ways the other person has been acting that are the reason for the boundary. But usually, the other person won't follow through because the response is more of an angry threat than a true boundary.

The response to all these challenges is essentially the same: to consistently and neutrally follow through with the consequences. That follow-through is what teaches the recipients that you honor and respect your own boundaries.

3. *The Recipient Chooses the Consequences*

One standard tool taught in counseling is the use of "I statements." They are a way to help people change patterns of blaming others and to help them take responsibility for themselves. Following through with boundaries is one of the few situations where I occasionally recommend clients use "you statements." These statements emphasize that the boundary recipients always choose the consequences. They choose to respect the limit or violate it, and by doing so, they choose the positive or negative consequences. If they don't like the consequences, they are always free to choose the other consequences with a different behavior.

As the boundary setter, it is your job to focus on what you do. Your role is to follow through with the consequences the other person chooses. In some circumstances, an appropriate response to someone testing the boundary may be, "You are choosing this consequence with your behavior." An even stronger way to put it, one which does more to neutralize the emotions, might be, "I'm following through with the consequences you chose." Most of the time, it isn't really necessary to say much at all. The action of consistently following through is the most effective form of communication. Essentially, when you follow through, you're telling the recipient, "If you don't like this consequence, choose the other one with your behavior."

For someone new to creating boundaries, the idea that the recipient chooses the consequences might seem like blaming. In fact, it is just the opposite. It is actually empowering because it clarifies that the boundary recipient has the freedom to choose. This shifts the relationship away from a previous disrespectful pattern of control and manipulation and makes room for more positive interactions that create respect and positive energy. By allowing boundary recipients to choose the consequences, they can take more responsibility for their actions and behaviors rather than the boundary setter taking on the recipients' responsibility.

4. *Separating Responsibility*

Another reason boundaries are so effective is that they make each person responsible and accountable only for his or her own behavior.

Your job as the boundary creator is to set the limit and establish the positive and negative consequences. The boundary recipient's job is to challenge and test the limit. Your job is to follow through with consequences. The recipient's job is to choose which consequences he or she wants to live with: the positive ones for respecting the limit or the negative ones for violating the limit. In essence, your job as the creator is to create change in the relationship; the recipient's job is to challenge that change to ensure that you, as the creator, are serious about the boundary and will have consistent follow-through. You are not responsible for the recipient's chosen behavior; you are only responsible for your own chosen behavior of following through with the consequences.

A pattern of punishments and rewards means the person setting the limit is maintaining control over and responsibility for the outcome. It creates resentment on both sides. Consequences, by contrast, kick in automatically based on the behavior chosen by the recipient. The emotions and potential for conflict are reduced because the consequences are appropriate, consistent, and have been clearly communicated. The decision point about the consequences came earlier; they are not being created during a moment of tension.

For the boundary setter, giving up control over the outcome can be very difficult. Just as the boundary recipients need to test the limits to learn to trust the person setting the limits, the boundary creator needs to practice consistent follow-through and letting go of control to learn that the recipients can be trusted with responsibility for their own actions.

Especially with children, allowing the boundary recipients to take responsibility for themselves teaches valuable life lessons. Not only do kids learn that their actions have consequences, but they also learn essential life skills and how to take care of themselves.

In our example of Lonnie and his children, here is how following through with consequences might look:

If Mark does the dishes on Monday, the family enjoys an evening free of tension or conflict over this particular chore. Lonnie doesn't praise Mark for doing the dishes, either. If he did, Lonnie would still be taking responsibility for Mark's behavior. The message communicated by the praise would be, "Thank you for doing this chore for me." Instead, letting the positive consequences speak for themselves allows Mark to be responsible for his own choice. Of course, if Mark does something above and beyond the typical chore of doing the dishes, an acknowledgment of appreciation is still appropriate.

If Mark doesn't do dishes on Monday, Lonnie doesn't nag or scold. He leaves the dishes alone and allows Mark to decide whether or not he will do his assigned chore.

If on Tuesday the dishes still are not done, Lonnie again leaves them to pile up in the kitchen. Again, he doesn't nag Mark or scold him.

Nor does he point out that Selena, who would usually do dishes on Tuesday, doesn't have to do them and is free to do other things instead. Mark can see for himself that his sister is getting out of her usual turn at this chore. This, in fact, is the piece that makes this particular consequence especially effective. I used this system with my own kids. What really encouraged them to comply was the knowledge that not only would they have to do an extra chore if they missed a day of doing dishes, but someone else would get to miss a turn. The idea that a sibling would get out of doing the dishes was enough motivation for the dishes to get done each day with no arguments or even discussions about the task.

Creating True Boundaries Takes Practice

Learning to establish boundaries is no different than learning any other new skill. It's best to start in small ways as you practice and build your skills and confidence. None of us can go from a pattern of being run over and accepting disrespect to a pattern of consistently following through with true boundaries in one easy step. You need to practice and learn, and in the process, you are bound to make mistakes.

A common mistake in the beginning is setting limits or consequences that aren't appropriate. When this happens, that doesn't mean you have failed or you can't create a boundary around that particular issue. It just means you need to revisit the boundary and set different limits or consequences.

An even more common mistake is not consistently following through with the consequences. Sometimes this happens because the consequences were not appropriate, and in that case, you can establish new consequences. Quite often, though, failing to follow through happens because you lapse back into old familiar patterns of allowing yourself to be treated with disrespect. Again, this isn't the end of creating boundaries around a given issue. It is just an opportunity to go back and reinstate the boundary. This gives you another chance to respect yourself by following through consistently. It's also another chance for the recipient to test the boundary and verify that you can be trusted to do what you say you will do.

The need to learn and practice is one reason it is wise to start creating boundaries around smaller, less emotional issues. It can be helpful to practice setting boundaries with people and situations you don't have strong emotional attachments to, such as coworkers. With significant people in your life, like family members, it's a good idea to begin establishing boundaries around relatively minor issues: doing dishes or laundry, maybe, rather than the intense emotionally abusive behavior.

Jackie had been married to Fred for two years when she first came in for marriage counseling. Jackie indicated that she and Fred had been in a relationship with each other four years prior to getting married, and they had a great relationship until they got married. After they got married, Jackie started to see a side of Fred that scared her. He was emotionally abusive and threatened her to the point that she felt afraid and trapped in the relationship.

Jackie was invited to bring Fred to a counseling session to discuss boundaries. Slowly, they established small boundaries that Jackie could safely follow through with. Within two years, Jackie established a number of boundaries that created safety for both of them and allowed Jackie to feel safer to speak her truth.

Beginning with smaller boundaries is a way to set yourself up for success with larger ones. When less emotion is involved, there is likely to be less confrontation or conflict over the boundary, so it is easier to succeed. This builds your confidence and your respect for yourself. It also teaches others that you can and will follow through. These small successes gradually create a habit on your part of establishing boundaries and a habit on the part of others of respecting those boundaries. One success at a time, you replace old patterns of disrespect and conflict with new patterns of mutual respect. As success is created with the smaller boundary issues, the stage is set to create boundaries for larger issues.

Chapter Four Reflections

While saying the right things and setting healthy and respectful limits with appropriate positive and negative consequences are critical for true boundaries, they are not boundaries unless there is 100 percent consistent follow through. If you cannot follow through with the positive and negative consequences associated with the limit 100 percent of the time with emotional neutrality, consequences may require modifications to achieve greater consistency.

Reflect on the limits and the positive and negative consequences you established in Chapters Two and Three.

Which ones present anger, vendettas, or grudges?

_____

_____

_____

Which of these limits and positive and negative consequences do you intend to explain more than once? If so, why?

_____

_____

_____

If a need to explain more than once exists, what can you change within yourself to decrease that need?

_____

_____

_____

The limits and positive and negative consequences indicated above are areas to go back and modify to prevent any of those obstacles from blocking success with the boundaries.

Which limits and positive and negative consequences are you prepared to consistently follow through with when they are tested?

Indicate on the chart below the anticipated level of testing with the boundaries you are establishing.

1 = no anticipated resistance   10 = excessive anticipated resistance

Boundaries	Anger Response	Accusing of Manipulation	Blame	Guilt	Making False Promises	Threats	Finding Loopholes	Setting Counter Boundaries

Comments or Reflections:

Practice by writing out and then sharing with a safe neutral person the way you intend to present these true boundaries to the recipients.

Which of these boundaries are you taking responsibility for?

_____

_____

_____

In which of these boundaries are you allowing the other person to choose the consequences and take responsibility for their actions?

_____

_____

_____

How True Boundaries Foster Mutual Respect

"Honoring your own boundaries is the clearest
message to others to honor them too."

— Gina Greenlee

The foundation of true, healthy boundaries is mutual respect. Or more precisely, fourfold respect or even respect squared. True mutual respect is more than just my respecting you and you respecting me. It also includes me respecting myself and you respecting yourself.

If I routinely tolerate abusive, rude, or otherwise disrespectful behavior from you, it's fairly obvious I'm not showing respect for myself. This lack of respect for myself ultimately encourages you to regard me disrespectfully. The two other aspects of "respect squared" are a bit less obvious, but just as important. If I allow you to run over me, I am showing a lack of respect for you. I am also fostering your own lack of respect for yourself.

True boundaries are respectful to the recipient as well as the creator. This is an important piece that some boundary-setting methods overlook. In many cases, it is implied that people with whom boundaries need to be set are "difficult," "bad," or somehow "the problem." Such an oversimplification misses two key points.

First, the purpose of true boundaries is to bring people closer together. Labeling someone as a "difficult" person who needs to be kept at a distance fails to do this. Instead, this labeling increases the distance in a relationship.

Second, in any relationship in which one person is consistently disrespectful to another, the behavior is part of a pattern that both parties have learned. Both of them have learned not to respect themselves and not to act with respect toward each other. The person who acts like a bully and the one who acts like a victim are carrying out complementary parts of the same pattern.

True Boundaries and Mutual Respect

The following stories illustrate some of the ways that allowing others to treat us disrespectfully shows a lack of respect for both ourselves and them. They also show how creating boundaries is respectful to both parties.

True Boundaries Allow Each Person to Change

Tolerating disrespectful behavior assumes the other person is unwilling to change or is incapable of changing, while it also assumes you are not worthy of more respectful treatment. Creating boundaries shows respect for yourself by setting limits, at the same time respecting the other person's right and responsibility to choose whether to comply with the boundary.

Mindy and Ray met when she began working as a secretary in the accounting firm where he was a CPA. She grew up in a small town where her parents owned a garbage collection business. He grew up in a city where his parents both taught at a university. Ray had a habit of making fun of Mindy's background in front of the couple's friends. He would make remarks like, "Mindy is my trash-pile treasure; I picked her up at the town dump," or "My mother-in-law doesn't own a junkyard dog; she is the junkyard dog."

Any time Mindy told Ray how much these "jokes" offended and hurt her, he would say, "Lighten up—I was just kidding." But there's always truth in this kind of barbed joke.

For years, Mindy, intimidated by her husband's higher level of education and what she saw as his sophistication, put up with his "kidding." This tolerance violated her own self-respect, and it also showed disrespect to Ray by allowing him to continue demonstrating his ignorance and bigotry. It denied him the opportunity to learn both about the reality and value of his in-laws' work and about more respectful behavior.

Eventually, Mindy created the following boundary: "As long as my parents and I are being respected in relationship to their profession, we can continue to connect and share. When I hear comments that are disrespectful of my parents and my family's background and work, I'll address it respectfully in front of the people hearing your criticism. I'll say something like, 'I feel hurt by your comment and I believe I deserve an apology.' I won't pretend it's a non-issue, and I won't wait until we're alone before I say something."

With this boundary, Mindy honored herself. She also showed respect for Ray by giving him the chance to change his disrespectful behavior with everyone involved at the time.

True Boundaries Resolve the Roles of Offender and Victim

Failing to create boundaries allows an opportunity to label the other person as bad or the problem. This is disrespectful to them because it fosters shame, guilt, and resentment on their part. It is disrespectful to you because it allows you to stay in a victim role instead of looking at your own part in the pattern. True boundaries interrupt the pattern of disrespectful behavior, rather than flipping it so the victim and the bully simply change roles. If you go from one extreme of being a victim to the other extreme of being a bully, that's not setting boundaries to create safety and respect; that's just a continuation of the same dysfunctional pattern with you and the other person switching roles.

Bruce had grown up in a quiet environment while his partner, Julian, had grown up with a lot of yelling and arguments. After several years together, Bruce was fed up with being yelled at. He felt bullied by Julian, not only because he was intimidated by Julian's volume, but also because the yelling included name-calling and disrespectful language. Bruce began counseling, where he was able to explore his history and his feelings about yelling. He recognized he was uncomfortable with noise, and also that yelling made him feel manipulated, controlled, and not heard. Julian insisted this was just his family's style of communicating and was not meant as controlling.

Bruce eventually set the boundary: "As long as there is no yelling, we will be able to effectively communicate in a positive fashion. If there is yelling, the conversation is over for half an hour. After that time-out, we will come back to the issue without yelling." Julian tested the boundaries repeatedly, even moving out for a short time. Bruce kept following through. Eventually, Julian realized he didn't like the yelling, either, and together the couple learned more respectful ways to communicate.

This example goes deeper than different styles of communicating. Quiet isn't always respectful, and noise isn't always disrespectful. Bruce also came to realize that his quiet family had done a lot of nonverbal "yelling" with silence and body language, which was just as disrespectful as the yelling in Julian's family. This realization helped him see beyond his initial perception of Julian as the bully and himself as the victim.

True Boundaries Foster Self-Reflection

The self-reflection that is an aspect of appropriate consequences encourages people to take responsibility for their actions instead of blaming. Punishment means people don't have to look at their own behavior; it gives them someone to blame. When we blame, we guilt and shame, which allows our emotional history and patterns to remain the same. Boundaries give ownership to the recipients and tend to shift the underlying uncomfortable feelings toward themselves, which invites self-reflection. It also leaves people their dignity instead of humiliating them.

Chelsea's first job after college was in a large company. Her supervisor, Mitch, was a married man nearly twice her age. He was friendly and treated her well, but after several months, his friendliness became inappropriate. There was nothing overtly sexual or harassing about it, but he began doing her favors, buying her small gifts, and finding excuses to call her at home. Chelsea liked her job and liked Mitch, but this behavior was unwelcome and made her uncomfortable. She told him it needed to end. He didn't change.

Chelsea talked to several other managers in the company and also researched the company's policies on sexual harassment. Then she wrote Mitch a letter setting out the limits she needed him to observe in his relationship with her, including no favors, gifts, or phone calls at home. She stated that if he complied, she wouldn't file a sexual harassment complaint and he wouldn't risk losing his job; work would go on as usual and they could maintain a healthy work relationship. If he did not comply, she would report his behavior as sexual harassment. The letter's tone was matter-of-fact and respectful, not threatening or angry.

Mitch chose to change his behavior.

With this boundary, Chelsea created safety for herself by bringing an end to the behavior that made her uncomfortable. She reinforced her sense of self-respect by taking care of herself in a mature way.

The boundary also increased safety and self-respect for Mitch. By dealing with his inappropriate behavior in its early stages, Chelsea offered him the chance to thoughtfully consider his behavior. She also gave him the opportunity to change his behavior before it led to a reprimand or a sexual harassment complaint. The two of them were able to continue a friendly working relationship until she left the job to further her career.

Enabling People to Continue Shame-Based Patterns

Not setting limits allows or encourages others to continue a learned behavior that violates their own deep emotional truth. True boundaries encourage reflection and awareness of the behavior in a non-shaming way, which can help facilitate change. Often, when people act in disrespectful ways, the behavior stems from their own experiences of being shamed and treated with disrespect. These experiences have taught them a pattern of not valuing or respecting themselves. Their own disrespectful actions continue the pattern of shaming, except that they may take the part of the perpetrator rather than the recipient. At some level, however, they may be aware that their behavior is disrespectful to their own true selves as well as to others. This awareness creates more shame, which only helps perpetuate the disrespectful pattern.

Alyssa fell on the ice and sprained her knee, which was still swollen and sore two days later. Her husband, Tyson, wanted sex that night. Alyssa told him no because she was too uncomfortable. He ignored her objections, insisting sex "would make her feel better." In line with the pattern they usually followed, she eventually gave in and allowed him to have sex, while she remained a passive and unresponsive partner. As usual, the encounter left both of them dissatisfied and resentful. Tyson felt ashamed of himself for insisting, and Alyssa felt ashamed of herself for giving in. These underlying sideways feelings were keeping both of them stuck in the disrespectful patterns they had learned from their past experiences.

Codependent Caretaking

Failing to create boundaries is codependent, controlling, and caretaking. True boundaries respectfully allow others to take responsibility for their own behavior. When you don't stand up to someone who is treating you with disrespect, you are taking care of that person emotionally. You may do this out of fear and a wish to protect yourself. You may also do it out of love, with the best of intentions to protect that person from pain. In either case, the result shows disrespect by treating the other person as a child who is not responsible for his or her own behavior. It fosters resentment on both sides.

Jolene and Gregg's son Brett, two years out of high school, had held a series of entry-level jobs and been fired several times. When he ended up jobless and homeless, his parents offered to let him move back in with them temporarily, with the understanding that he would help with household chores, look for a job, and work to get back on his feet. By the end of the third week, Brett had not taken any steps toward finding a job. He was sleeping till noon, spending most of his time watching TV or playing video games, and not even picking up after himself.

By tolerating this behavior, Gregg and Jolene were treating themselves with disrespect by allowing their generosity to be taken advantage of. The situation was also disrespectful to Brett. He was being treated like a dependent child rather than an adult capable of taking care of himself, and he was enabled to continue a pattern of self-destructive behavior.

Eventually, Jolene and Gregg created the following boundaries:

- As long as Brett is actively seeking employment, he can live at home for a maximum of six months only. At the end of that time, he will move out. If Brett chooses to continue sitting around and is not actively hunting for or engaged in a job, he will be choosing to leave earlier than the six-month deadline and find a different place to live.

- Four evenings a week, Brett will attend classes at a career education center to improve his job skills until he finds a secure job. If Brett chooses not to participate in the classes and does not have a job, he will be choosing to leave and find a different place to live.

- Brett will get up by 7:00 a.m. By getting up by 7:00, Brett is choosing to connect with the family before they go to work. If he chooses to get up later, he is choosing to allow family members to come into his room, turn the lights on, open the curtains, and wake him.

- Brett will spend a minimum of four hours each day actively job-hunting. Actively job-hunting means preparing a resume for the types of jobs he hopes to obtain, completing applications, doing follow-up calls, setting up and participating in interviews, sending thank-you notes for the interviews, and continuing to follow up until the company makes a decision about his employment. This process will help Brett focus and give him purpose for moving forward. If Brett chooses not to participate in the job-hunting process, he will be choosing to leave and find a different place to live.

- Brett will mow the yard once a week and help with housework as specified on a posted daily chore chart. Participating in household chores is part of living in this house. To help focus on chores, home electronic devices are available only after the chores are completed.

- Brett will do his own laundry and put it away. Taking care of his laundry means he will have clean clothes he can find when he needs them. Failing to do his laundry means he chooses to wear dirty clothes.

- Once he finds a job, Brett will pay rent at $150 per week in preparation for moving into his own apartment at the end of the six-month period. As long as these boundaries are maintained and Brett maintains his employment until the end of his six-month stay, he will be entitled to 75 percent of the rent back to go toward a deposit and rent for his new apartment. If he chooses not to pay the rent, he chooses to leave. If Brett leaves earlier than planned due to any form of boundary violation described above, he is choosing to give up his rent money as well.

Cycles of Resentment and Punishment

Lack of true boundaries fosters disrespectful behavior such as manipulation, secrets, and getting even. Boundaries encourage respectful, clear communication. When someone is punished out of anger, rather than being allowed to experience consequences that are emotionally neutral and have been communicated in advance, that person will most likely respond with anger. The result is a cycle of resentment and more punishment from both sides. Even those who lack the power to punish back directly, such as children or employees, will find ways to get revenge. The emotional neutrality of true boundaries, on the other hand, takes much of the energy and resentment out of the interaction.

Abbie, new to her job in a real estate appraisal firm, prepared a report for a client that contained several errors. Her boss, George, didn't review the report before giving it to the client during a meeting. When the mistakes were discovered, George called Abbie into his office and, in front of the client, scolded her harshly for being careless. Abbie left the office in tears. The next day, she started looking for another job. In the meantime, she didn't bother to correct mistakes, "forgot" to give George his phone messages, and was rude to clients. For years afterward, Abbie never missed an opportunity to say something negative about George.

Eileen, in a similar situation with a new boss, was called into his office because he was angry about something that had gone wrong. He began shouting and swearing at her. Eileen stood up, said, "It's not okay for you to talk to me like that," and walked out. A short time later, her boss came to her desk and apologized. The two eventually developed a close, respectful working relationship, and twenty years later Eileen still worked for him and was one of his most valued employees.

Negative Attention

A lack of boundaries creates negative attention, which may take the form of arguments, shouting, scolding, or power struggles. In the midst of this kind of chaos, people are unable to genuinely notice one another. True boundaries provide respectful attention in several ways: The limits provide appropriate attention to the boundary recipient and make clear that the boundary setter wants to be noticed respectfully; the consequences get the recipient's attention without shaming or blaming; and following through with emotional neutrality removes the negative attention on both sides.

In the example described in Chapter One with Naomi's grandson Tony visiting for the summer, Tony's initial method of testing the boundaries was to escalate the level of confrontation, with a lot of screaming and yelling. Instead of engaging with him and giving him negative attention in response, Naomi stayed emotionally neutral. She respectfully allowed Tony to discharge his emotions with what was essentially a temper tantrum that began with anger and reached a point of tears. After Tony's emotions were discharged, he and his grandmother were able to connect and discuss the issue at hand. This gave Tony attention from Naomi in a positive and appropriate way.

We all need attention, and if we are used to negative attention, that's what we will look for. Following through neutrally with consequences both reduces the negative attention and models the alternative of more positive attention.

Distance

Lack of true boundaries creates more distance in a relationship, while true boundaries bring people closer by fostering mutual respect. This respect doesn't necessarily mean two people become close friends;

it may just allow them to work together more comfortably.

Vince worked in a cubicle in a small insurance company. A coworker, Ed, had a habit of stopping in with his mid-morning cup of coffee and making himself comfortable in the visitors' chair for a leisurely chat. While Vince enjoyed talking with Ed, he grew increasingly frustrated and angry over having his time wasted. Yet he didn't know how to stop Ed's visits.

One day, Vince poured water over the seat of the visitor's chair. Ed came by as usual and dropped into the chair. As the water soaked into the seat of his pants, he stopped talking in mid-sentence, then abruptly jumped up and fled back to his own cubicle. He never dropped in again.

Since Vince's strategy accomplished what he wanted, which was to keep Ed from interrupting him, was it a good solution? Not at all. Instead of increasing safety, respect, and closeness, it decreased all three. The practical joke was a disrespectful punishment that humiliated Ed. It was also disrespectful to Vince. He found it funny, but it also left him feeling ashamed of himself. It created distance and tension between the two men.

How might Vince have created a boundary to end Ed's interruptions in a respectful way? The key would be to focus on the time-management aspect of the situation and politely not engage with Ed.

Here's one example: Ed comes in with his coffee and sits down as usual. Vince says, "I have two minutes; then I have to make a phone call." He visits with Ed for two minutes, then says, "I guess our time's up," and picks up his phone. Or Vince says, "I really don't have time to talk this morning. Let's get together for lunch instead. Does tomorrow work for you?" After making the lunch appointment, he says, "See you then," and shifts his attention back to his work.

In either example, Ed's negative consequence for disregarding the limit would be sitting in Vince's office without receiving Vince's attention. The positive consequence for respecting the limit would be having Vince's full attention for two minutes or having a chance to talk comfortably over lunch.

Such a boundary would reduce Vince's resentment, without shifting the resentment to Ed by punishing him. It would foster self-respect and closeness for both men by offering an opportunity to build their friendship without wasting their employer's time.

§§§§§

A lack of boundaries creates a murky environment of mixed messages, unspoken expectations, and tension. People often don't know what the rules and expectations are until they violate one, and then the infraction may be punished at times and ignored at other times. Clear true boundaries, on the other hand, create clarity in communication and expectations. With true boundaries, both people in the relationship are acting in the light, in full view.

True boundaries foster integrity and respect on both sides. When you create true boundaries, you say what you mean and mean what you say. Following through with consequences is keeping a commitment to yourself. With true boundaries, you treat yourself as a person worthy of keeping your word, and you treat others as people worth keeping your word to. Creating true boundaries is acting respectfully toward yourself and others. It is a recognition that, as human beings, we are all equal and all worthy of respect.

Chapter Five Reflections

Increased respect, safety, and trust are fruits of true boundaries. If these fruits are not present and growing, it is time to reflect on the established limits, positive and negative consequences, and 100 percent follow-through to see what is hampering your success.

This chapter was about self-respect that facilitates self-reflection when the boundary is not working as intended. Are the consequences for the limit appropriate in creating the appropriate change? Are the consequences facilitating or fostering resentments or controlling and hampering the process?

If the consequences are emotionally appropriate with no control, then it is important to explore the follow-through. Many times people share that the boundary will not work because the other person will not follow through with the consequences. It is not the other person's responsibility to follow through; it is your responsibility.

Choose one of your boundaries. List the ways this boundary will bring you closer to the person you are setting the boundary with:

Are you bullying or feeling bullied with this boundary you have established?

_____

_____

_____

If either party is feeling bullied, reflect on how the boundary was presented. Is the boundary framed so the other person realizes they have a choice of consequences? If not, reframe the limit's consequences.

_____

_____

_____

Is the other person bullying you by totally ignoring the boundary? Reflect on the consequences and adjust them so you can consistently follow through. Verify that the consequences are capable of gaining respect from the other person.

_____

_____

_____

Verify that the other person has two options you can follow through with and that the options create an opportunity for change. List the options below.

_____

_____

_____

What are you learning about yourself with these boundaries?

_____

_____

_____

Choose one of your boundaries. Explain how the boundary is helping create either more respect or more shame-based patterns:

Explain where any codependent behaviors are interfering with the boundary.

_____

_____

_____

List any resentments or punishment patterns that may be present with the boundaries.

_____

_____

_____

List any negative attention the boundaries may be creating.

_____

_____

_____

List the ways the boundaries may be creating distance or respect in the relationship.

_____

_____

_____

THE CHALLENGE OF FOLLOWING THROUGH WITH TRUE BOUNDARIES

"Setting boundaries is a way of caring for myself. It doesn't make me mean, selfish, or uncaring…."

— Christine Morgan

The benefits of having true boundaries in place are huge: less conflict, more emotional and physical safety, more comfortable family functioning, clearer communication, greater respect, more emotional closeness, stronger relationships, and more loving relationships. These benefits make life much more comfortable and satisfying for both the creator of true boundaries and their recipient.

Nor is the process of creating true boundaries all that complicated. The three steps covered in Chapters Two through Four—setting limits, establishing positive and negative consequences, and following through consistently with those consequences—are quite straightforward. Just because the process is relatively easy to understand, however, doesn't mean it is easy to carry out.

I've worked with many people who tell me they want to set boundaries. They realize it would improve their relationships and foster their own self-respect. They understand that boundaries are valuable. Yet relatively few of them succeed at creating and maintaining true boundaries.

Why are boundaries such a challenge? Because there are as many obstacles as there are benefits to setting boundaries. These obstacles can be loosely divided into four categories: fear, ignorance, negative payoffs, and codependency. The categories overlap and are not rigid divisions. They are a convenient way to help understand our difficulties with setting boundaries. Let's take a closer look at each one.

Fear

Fear is one of the greatest obstacles to setting boundaries. Here are just some of the fears most of us have that block our ability to set and maintain true boundaries:

1. *Fear of looking like the "bad guy"*

One common response from clients when we talk about boundaries is some variation of, "But if I set boundaries, people won't like me." When I emphasize the importance of consistently following through with consequences, people sometimes say, "But you're so hard," "You are too rigid," or "That's so harsh." As long as we don't challenge the status quo by setting boundaries, we can hold on to the perception that others like us because we are "nice." What we don't realize is that people who need and expect us to always be "nice"—in other words, cooperative or submissive—don't respect us. When our need to be nice makes us afraid to stand up for ourselves, we are not showing respect for ourselves, and we don't receive respect from others.

It is true, however, that anyone who starts changing the patterns in a relationship by creating boundaries will probably be seen as "the bad guy" for a time. This is especially true in families if one parent starts implementing boundaries with children and the other doesn't.

Kathy felt unheard and disrespected when she set boundaries around chores with her children Connor and Hanna. Rather than comply with the boundaries, they would call their dad "Rick." He would pick them up and take them to his house, which allowed him to look like the good parent. Kathy realized she needed to set a boundary with Rick. She did so as follows: "The children may not go to your house outside of the regular visitation schedule unless you arrange that visit with me. If the kids call you, and you come to get them without my permission, I won't let them go. If you respect the limit by telling Connor and Hanna you won't come get them, life will go on as usual. If you show up at my house in violation of the limit, if necessary I will ask Loren and Pat (close neighbors who were Kathy's good friends and supporters) to come over to support me. If they are not available, I will call the police."

Initially, even though Rick respected the limit, he and the children all made Kathy out to be the bad person. As she consistently followed through with the consequences in both her boundary with Rick and her boundaries with Connor and Hanna, the resistance decreased. Kathy's respectful consistency helped Hanna and Connor feel more comfortable, to the point that they no longer needed or desired to call their dad to intervene.

Parents who overcome the fear of being the bad guy and persist in following through with boundaries will ultimately develop a closer and more respectful relationship with their kids, even if in the short term, they are seen as the mean parents. I have seen this in my own life and with families I have worked with. Children not only need boundaries; they want them and want the safer, more respectful environments that true boundaries create.

2. Fear of hurting the other person

We may be afraid that if we set boundaries, other people will be upset. They might feel hurt, or cry, or withdraw. They might think we don't love them. Our boundaries might drive them away. This fear is a codependent need to take care of others. We have the perception that their feelings are more important than our own, so we try to take care of them at the cost of our own self-respect.

Albert was a quiet and reserved person who had learned to use his quietness as a way to control his wife, Roberta. Roberta wanted to establish a boundary with Albert that would allow them both to look at a number of issues they had a pattern of avoiding. When the topic of finances would come up, for example, Albert would get defensive and quiet, then end the conversation and leave. Roberta felt frustrated, and she was still afraid to set a boundary. Her fear was that the boundary would decrease the little connection she and Albert had. Not creating the boundary only intensified her feelings of loneliness and abandonment.

3. Fear of conflict or confrontation

Fear of conflict or confrontation is also common. We are afraid that if we set boundaries and upset others, they might scold, punish, or attack us. This fear is especially strong for those who have been taught, often through physical or emotional abuse, that it is dangerous to do anything that might anger others. Being careful not to rock the boat allows us to "walk on egg shells" or live in constant anxiety and to hold on to the belief that we are safe. People with this belief may take a long time to reach a point of realizing, "I have to create boundaries to protect and respect myself." It can be hard to accept the reality that the "safety" created by having no boundaries is not real. Even though boundaries may increase conflict in the short term, they reduce confrontation and conflict in the long term. Boundaries are about truth-telling and honesty, which promote genuine safety rather than the illusion of safety.

When anger and physical abuse are part of the relationship, it can be terrifying to set a boundary because the triggers for these violent patterns can be unpredictable. Ellen was in such a relationship with her partner, Ron. It took more than two years of encouragement and processing with a counselor for her to start the process of change by creating a small boundary. Ellen decided to set the limit with Ron that she would no longer accept his negative comments toward her. If she received no negative comments, life would go on as usual. If Ron made negative comments, Ellen would leave the room and not engage until a sincere formal written apology was given. If Ellen felt that remaining in the house would be unsafe, she made arrangements to go stay with her best friend Jackie until the sincere formal apology was given.

4.   *Fear of the change and effort that learning to set boundaries requires*

It is much easier to stay in a familiar pattern of feeling resentful and blaming others for taking advantage of you than it is to do the work of recovery and change. If you want to be respected, it is important you learn to respect yourself, take responsibility for yourself, be emotionally present, and develop emotional maturity. All of this growth takes commitment, time, and plain old hard work.

Establishing boundaries where no boundaries have existed in the past is scary and difficult because it is unfamiliar. The fear of changing what is familiar, even if the familiar is hurtful or abusive, can overpower most desires for change because the change is unfamiliar and scary. Creating safety in a relationship with true boundaries means you face your fears to do something unfamiliar. For example, Eva was feeling anxious and resentful with her roommate, Jill. Eva liked having a clean kitchen so that the dishes were available when they were needed. Jill liked leaving the dirty dishes in the kitchen sink and doing them when she had time. The dishes were creating tension in the relationship, yet Eva was afraid to address the issue because of Jill's anger. Eva was able to see that the anger reminded her of her dad's anger, which she had been unable to stand up to because to do so only meant that the anger would get worse. When Eva was able to work through these feelings of fear, she was able to set a boundary with Jill.

5. *Fear of admitting that something is wrong in the relationship*

Sometimes the first obstacle to creating boundaries you need to overcome is your own denial. A crucial step in learning to set true boundaries is developing enough respect for yourself to admit the reality that a relationship is not what you would like it to be.

Beth had dreamed of living the ideal life in an ideal relationship with the husband of her dreams. While she and her husband, Leo, both wanted everyone to think their marriage was perfect, their friends could see the shortcomings and would often mention them to Beth. It seemed the harder Beth worked to make their relationship look perfect, the easier it was for her friends to find the faults and vocalize the uncomfortable feelings she was attempting to hide. For Beth, the fear of seeing her relationship as anything less than perfect was devastating.

6. *Fear of disrupting the familiar pattern of interactions in the family or the relationship*

This fear may take the form of being afraid that you will set boundaries and fail because others won't respect them. But it's just as likely to be a fear that you will set boundaries and succeed because others will comply with them. Either way, the patterns of behavior you have learned to follow will change. Those patterns may not feel safe or nurturing, but they are what you are used to, and you know how they work. Even if setting boundaries changes those patterns for the better, the process will be uncomfortable and will take you into unfamiliar territory.

As described in number three above, Ellen was initially terrified at the idea of creating a boundary with Ron. Yet the intensity of fear associated with his anger motivated her either to set the boundary or run where he would not find her. Ellen had much to lose if she ran, so she decided the boundary would be less traumatic for her to try. When she set the boundary, Ron immediately started to cut her down with negative comments because that was the typical response he was familiar with to control her. When Ellen left the room, Ron immediately followed her, at which time she called her friend, Jackie, who came right over to pick her up.

Because Ron was filled with fear and anger, he decided to follow Ellen to Jackie's house. When they realized he was following them, the women called the police, who met them at Jackie's house. The police were able to defuse the situation and Ron went home.

Ron refused to write the apology letter for two days, so Ellen and Jackie were able to have a nice time connecting. After the second day, Ron was feeling lonely enough that he conceded and wrote the apology letter, and Ellen came back home.

The next time Ron started to cut down Ellen, she left the room again and ended back with Jackie. This pattern slowly decreased in intensity and frequency until Ellen no longer needed to leave the home. In the process, Ellen and Ron's ability to communicate in a positive manner improved, and slowly, the relationship improved.

7. *Fear of losing what you have that is tied to the relationship*

In some cases, the fears you have around setting boundaries are not so much about the person you need to set boundaries with as they are about your circumstances that may be affected by that person. "If I tell my boss it's not okay to call me 'sweetie,' I might lose my job." "If I resign from the board of the service club because the president is so unreasonable, I might lose my friendships in the club."

8. *Fear of losing the relationship*

Fear of losing a relationship is a huge fear and one of the biggest obstacles to setting true boundaries. Essentially, it comes down to this: "If I insist on being treated with respect, you might not love me anymore. You might leave."

A major part of this obstacle is the fear that the disrespectful behavior I want you to change might mean more to you than I do. If I set a boundary regarding that behavior, you might choose the behavior over me. You might not love me enough to respect the boundary.

The difficult truth is that if the other person in a relationship is being abusive or disrespectful, at least for now that person has already chosen the disrespectful behavior over the relationship. This is especially obvious in the case of someone with an addiction. Suppose Kayla, an alcoholic, has a pattern of getting drunk, showing up at her sister Nikki's house, and talking and crying for hours about how unhappy she is and how badly everyone treats her. Finally, Nikki has enough and sets this limit: "Our relationship is important to me, and I want to have open communication, which we can have when no alcohol is involved. If you come to my house when you're drunk, I won't let you in. If you stand there banging on the door and shouting, I will call the cops."

When Kayla tests the limit by showing up drunk and refusing to leave, Nikki follows through by calling the police. Kayla's response is to cut off contact with her sister. She chooses alcohol over the relationship. Her behavior says that her addiction is more important than her sister.

If you set limits, and the other person refuses to respect them, chances are you already are getting very little that is healthy or respectful in the relationship. Even if that is the case, though, the fear of losing what little you do have is enormous. It's common that people in abusive relationships have been emotionally abandoned as children. One of their biggest fears as adults is being abandoned again. This leads them to hang on to relationships and accept disrespect, emotional abuse, and physical abuse rather than risk the other person leaving. Many times, people in these circumstances will learn about boundaries, talk about boundaries, and even set limits, but they are unable to follow through because the fear of losing the other person is so great.

However, just because someone chooses a substance or behavior over you does not always mean the choice is permanent. When you learn to set true boundaries and follow through consistently, eventually the other person will probably get it. Because you learn to treat yourself with respect by setting boundaries, the other person is likely to learn to respect you as well.

The risk, of course—and it's a very real risk, especially when addictions are involved—is that the relationship might end. The addict may continue to choose the addiction. When you come to value yourself, you are no longer willing to tolerate disrespectful behavior. Eventually, you may realize that you no longer need to hold on to a relationship that gives you so little.

Because fear is such a strong barrier, a prerequisite for creating successful boundaries is to build your ability to move through that fear. Most of us have learned patterns of punishments and rewards, which build anger and resentment, rather than limits and consequences, which neutralize anger. If that's what you are used to, you will expect others to react with anger when you set limits. It takes courage and practice, starting with small issues, to act in spite of your fears and create patterns more respectful of yourself and of others.

Ignorance

Another major barrier to setting true boundaries is simple ignorance. You don't create effective boundaries because you don't know how. Setting boundaries is a learned skill, and it's one very few of us were taught. Most of us have not been taught to set true boundaries and have not experienced true boundaries. Instead, we start very early to learn about all the disrespectful behaviors described in Chapter One that are not boundaries: punishments and rewards, walls, nagging, manipulation, threats, and ultimatums.

In too many environments, disrespect—for both yourself and others—is actually rewarded. When parents reward children with praise like, "You're so brave for not crying," the children learn they are expected to hide their true feelings. When, in some daycare centers and classrooms, groups of children are "managed" in ways that disregard their individual needs or ideas, the children learn to discount themselves. Our adversarial court system shows us that hostility and "gotcha" tactics are the way to win. Many of our laws, from traffic regulations to criminal codes, are based on punishments and control rather than respect and education. Even what our society and culture teach as polite behavior can be disrespectful when it emphasizes pretense and getting along with others at the expense of honesty and self-respect.

This emphasis on punishments and rewards teaches chaos and confusion, not respect. It's no wonder, then, that we find it so hard to speak up for ourselves and behave with respect for ourselves as well. We want respect, but we may be terrified of it because it's unfamiliar.

Learning to set true boundaries is not much different from learning algebra or how to play the piano. You need to learn the process and start with small, easy tasks before you take on more difficult ones, and you need to practice.

Learning to set boundaries differs from learning other skills in one important way: Since so many people have no history with boundaries, others don't know how to respect boundaries any more than you—or they don't know how to create them. Chances are that most of the people around you don't know any more about boundaries than you do, so you need to teach them. When you learn to set boundaries, then, you are teaching others about boundaries at the same time you are creating safety for yourself. This teaching comes through your consistency in following through with consequences.

Negative Payoffs

Living without true boundaries has so many negative aspects, like chaos, resentment, and confusion, that someone on the outside might wonder why anyone would stay in such a situation. One answer is that both the person who fails to set boundaries and the person who violates boundaries get something from the relationship. Negative payoffs make up another major obstacle to setting boundaries. Typically, neither person is consciously aware of these negative payoffs because they usually hurt and have no obvious positive aspects. The payoffs are not deliberately chosen and are part of disrespectful patterns both people have learned.

Many people struggle with the idea that negative payoffs are actually a payoff since they see a payoff as something positive. Our subconscious is unaware of the payoff as being positive or negative; it is just a payoff. When you engage in a negative pattern, the payoff will also be negative.

Here are some typical negative payoffs:

1. *Attention*

Suppose Lily, age five, has been told that bedtime is 8:00 p.m., but her parents don't have a bedtime routine or consistent consequences for being or not being in bed on time. She has learned to whine or coax them to let her stay up later, to dawdle over brushing her teeth and getting into her pajamas, and to come up with one excuse after another to stay up longer or get out of bed once she's there. The payoff for Lily is her parents' attention of yelling, screaming, and criticizing. True, it's probably negative attention, because eventually they're going to get mad, but it's still attention. Lily is also being taught that she needs to whine, manipulate, and nag to get what she wants or needs.

Children aren't the only ones who get attention this way. The employee who constantly interrupts coworkers with "just one quick question" that is more than just the question might also be getting the negative payoff of negative attention. So might people who tell inappropriate jokes, invade others' personal space, or constantly show up late.

2. Engagement

Engagement is similar to getting attention, but it is more of a pattern between people who have no boundaries with each other. Tina and Gary, for example, had been married for fifteen years when they began counseling. Their relationship consisted mostly of a pattern of fighting and making up. Disrespect and conflict were the only ways they knew how to relate to each other.

Gary would get mad because Tina was late getting home from work, or Tina would start shouting because Gary changed the TV channel in the middle of a program she was watching. Every few days, something minor would trigger a loud argument, during which they swore at and threatened each other. Then, in the second phase of the pattern, they would refuse to speak to each other for a day or so. The third phase was making up. Tina would buy Gary a music CD, or Gary would cook Tina's favorite dessert, and they would both apologize, say how much they loved each other, and go to bed for passionate sex.

Gary and Tina repeated this cycle over and over, until they finally got tired of it and sought out counseling. The counseling helped them see that their pattern of adrenaline and drama was a sideways manner of expressing emotions because neither of them had ever learned to share their feelings in healthy ways.

3. Control

Control is a way of managing fear and anxiety. When you control relationships, though, you actually create distance and resentment. If Marti is nagging and fussing at her children every day about doing their homework, who is in charge of their behavior? She is. She is holding on to control over and responsibility for what they do. Instead of respecting her kids enough to allow them to choose their behavior and learn from the consequences, she is micro-managing, trying to make sure they do what she wants them to do. Her intent is loving: She wants what is best for her kids, which includes having them do their homework so they learn and get good grades. Yet in trying to take care of them in this way, Marti is actually treating them with disrespect. She is unconsciously communicating to them that she doesn't trust them to be responsible for their own behavior. Marti is also teaching her children not to be responsible for themselves and to resent her control.

Suppose instead Marti creates a clear boundary around homework:

Limit: "Homework is to be done as soon as you come home from school and have had a snack. There will be no electronics (TV, video games, computer, or phone) other than computer use required for any homework, no friends over, and no other distractions until the homework is finished."

Positive consequence: "When homework is completed, you can choose to use your electronics or spend time with friends."

Negative consequence: "As long as the homework is not completed, you are choosing not to use your electronics or spend time with you friends."

This boundary raises the question of how Marti will know when the homework is finished. The children are responsible for showing that the homework is completed, and verify that it is both completed and turned in. If a serious problem occurs with a child not turning in homework, she may need to regularly check on the school website with the child, or ask teachers to sign off to confirm receiving the work.

An approach that has been quite effective, especially if it is established as a habit when children are young, is to set a given time each evening to go over homework. This plan not only verifies that assignments are done, but can provide positive attention.

For Marti to follow up in this way may seem to be controlling. Yet it is not. She is not taking responsibility for doing the homework, but she is taking responsibility for following through with the consequences if it is done or not done. The responsibility for and control over whether the homework is done rests with the children. They are free to do it or not, and to choose the consequences either way.

As kids get older, what constitutes appropriate limits and consequences around issues like homework will change. It is also important to create appropriate boundaries based on different children's individual issues and needs. The key is to be consistent with boundaries when children are young so the pattern is well-established by the time they are teenagers.

Creating boundaries means relinquishing control to the other person, while giving them a choice; however, giving up control is a big obstacle for many of us. The need to control is based on fear, which shows up in various ways. "If I don't do it, it won't get done," or "They won't do it right," or "Things will fall apart," or "If I don't make sure this happens, I'll be a bad parent." Having no boundaries equals lots of fear, which fosters the need to control and leads to behavior like nagging or interfering with natural consequences.

4. *Blaming and being the victim*

Blaming and being the victim is another negative payoff based on fear. Sylvia felt belittled and bullied by her older brother Lucas, especially when it came to caring for their elderly father. Lucas's name was first on their father's power of attorney, and Lucas made medical and financial decisions for their father without consulting Sylvia. Then he would call and tell her what help he expected from her, such as taking their father to medical appointments or providing meals.

Sylvia felt like unpaid help instead of a partner in taking care of their father. Yet she wasn't able to set limits with her brother. In part, this inability was because she was intimidated by him, and Sylvia also was getting a negative payoff. As long as she could blame Lucas for not listening to her, not respecting her, or not changing, the negative payoff was that she didn't have to accept responsibility. She didn't have to participate in the hard decisions about their father's care, but she could criticize the decisions her brother made. She could be the victim, the "good guy," while Lucas was the bully or the "bad guy."

Blame is a major obstacle to setting boundaries. It helps keep you stuck in unhealthy patterns without having to change or to look at yourself and your part in those patterns. You feed blame when you tell yourself things like, "They'll never follow through," or "They won't listen to me anyway." A negative consequence of blame is shame. Both you and the person you blame receive some shame when you blame. Since blame typically is an inherent pattern you have been taught, you typically do not recognize the shame associated with it.

5. *Staying with what's familiar*

As long as you can maintain the status quo and not rock the boat, your environment doesn't change. This stagnation gives you an illusion of safety and the payoff of staying stuck in what's familiar. It also allows you to avoid the effort of learning to set and follow through with true boundaries. Instead, you can take the familiar and apparently easier path of trying to believe that the way things are is good enough. You can continue to pretend not to notice or care that you are being treated with disrespect—both by those around you and by yourself.

Owen resented and was hurt by the way his parents expected him to do all the work in their relationship. They never called him, and they expected him to call them at least once a week. If he didn't arrange visits or make plans for holidays and special occasions, the family didn't get together. The relationship felt lopsided, with Owen running after his parents and being the "doer." This wasn't because his parents were elderly or incapacitated; it was the pattern that had marked the relationship ever since Owen left home. Despite his resentment, Owen continued to do all the calling and planning to stay in contact with his parents because the pattern was so familiar. Staying with what he knew felt safe and easy, so he tolerated the disrespect of the situation.

The need to stay with what is familiar keeps both parties stuck in a pattern of mutual disrespect for which they share responsibility. Sometimes people will say something like, "My partner is being so mean and I want to change that," or "I need to change." Yet they aren't ready to take action because they have the intellectual knowledge that the pattern isn't working and not the deeper emotional readiness to change.

Someone may also ask, "Why do I have to do all the work?" The answer is, "You're the only one you can change, and since the level of discomfort resides in you, the energy and motivation to do the work that will create the change is in you." That effort isn't "doing all the work," it's "doing all *your* work." It's taking responsibility for your part of the pattern and choosing to change it by acting with respect for yourself.

The more often you repeat the disrespectful patterns you have learned, the more you will receive the "reward" of negative payoffs. These unconscious payoffs may be rewards, but they are sideways rewards that create negative outcomes and keep you stuck. It may be difficult to see negative patterns as payoffs; the important piece about them is the word "negative." The payoffs may be negative, hurtful, and even disrespectful, but what makes them payoffs is being able to stay in a familiar pattern.

Codependency

The fundamental obstacle to creating boundaries, one that underlies all the others, is codependency. Here is a brief definition of codependency taken from my book *Finding Emotional Freedom*:

> The term codependency was originally coined to describe someone married to or in a close relationship with an addict. Addiction professionals and treatment centers referred to the person with chemical dependency as the "dependent," and then to the spouse as the "co-dependent." The word has evolved to refer to anyone with a dysfunctional focus on the needs of others that goes beyond being concerned about or caring for them. Codependent behavior includes trying to control others, taking care of others in ways that interfere with their own responsibility to take care of themselves, and focusing on others to the extent of failing to take care of ourselves. When we are acting out in a codependent way, we believe we are helping, but we may actually be doing just the opposite....
>
> Codependency is when we place the needs of others before our

own and, deep down, we desire some form of recognition for what we do or have some form of resentment about it. If we could look deeply enough within ourselves, we would find some resentment around taking care of others. When we hurt ourselves or others in any way by placing others' needs above our own, the sideways resentment appears. Some of the forms it may take include feeling like martyrs or victims, expecting to be acknowledged for our sacrifices (even though no one asked us to make them), passive/aggressive behavior, sideways anger, or keeping score. The resentment may or may not be conscious, and it may not be large, yet it is there....

Another aspect of codependency is feeling a sense of responsibility for people, actions, or outcomes that are not legitimately our responsibility. Even when we don't take action, we may care or worry more about something than does the person in charge of it. Sometimes our need to take care of others is not wanted and may even hinder another person. This is where codependency becomes very apparent. The attitude might be summed up as, "I am going to do this for you whether you like it or not, so you will appreciate what I do for you."

If you want to learn more about codependency, its development, its impact, and the process of recovery, you will find that information in *Finding Emotional Freedom*. Codependency as it relates specifically to boundaries, however, can be defined more narrowly:

Codependency is a false belief that we must put other people's emotions, needs, and wants ahead of our own. We have some resentment about this, and we continue to act as if our own feelings and needs are secondary because we have been taught that we don't matter.

Certainly, at times, it's appropriate to put others' emotions, needs, or wants ahead of our own. Just ask any parent who has ever been up half the night with a hungry baby or a sick child. Behavior like this isn't codependency; it's responsible parenting. It is a choice to temporarily set aside our own needs and wants to take care of someone else's legitimate needs.

Codependency, in contrast, isn't a conscious situational choice. It's a default position, a learned mindset that other people always matter more than you do. You are taught to put others' emotions, needs, and wants first, even at the cost of discounting and being disrespectful to yourself. This false belief hides a deep emotional truth: the knowledge that you do matter and you are worthy of the same respect as others. At an unconscious level you realize this truth, and it is the source of the resentment that is an inherent part of codependency.

Codependency is a significant obstacle to creating boundaries. When you follow a codependent pattern of believing that others matter more than you do, you aren't only being disrespectful to yourself and allowing others to treat you disrespectfully. You also put others in a one-up position and yourself in a one-down position, which means you always come in second. To stay in second place, you need someone else to be first. The other person in a relationship—whether it's a spouse, parent, child, friend, or boss—has to be there to fill the one-up position in the pattern. You don't know how to be or act outside of that pattern, which is what you have learned and what you know. So you are terrified of doing anything that might upset that person enough to cause him or her to disrupt the familiar pattern.

This is the underlying source of many of the fears described earlier in this chapter. It is also why one of the most common objections I hear when I talk with clients about boundaries is, "But they'll be upset." Believing we need to live life in such a way that we don't upset anyone is actually another way to describe codependency.

Creating boundaries means becoming willing to allow the other person to be upset short term to create more safety, respect, cooperation, and comfort for everyone long term. It's a lot like choosing between living with the pain of a chronic toothache or going to the dentist to get the tooth taken care of. The toothache may not be severe, but it's a constant low level of pain. You may tolerate the pain for several reasons: it's so familiar you don't remember what it's like to live without it, it's endurable even though it hurts, and you are afraid to face what you think will be the greater pain of having the tooth fixed. Yet a visit to the dentist, even though it could possibly be more painful in the short term, will provide the lasting benefit of freedom from chronic pain. In the same way, moving through the temporary increase in conflict that may come with setting boundaries offers the lasting benefit of greatly reducing chronic conflict.

§§§§§

While the obstacles to creating true boundaries—fear, ignorance, negative payoffs, and codependency—are certainly real, they are not insurmountable. Admittedly, overcoming them isn't easy. Yet it can be done, with courage, effort, and a commitment to your own self-respect and safety.

One valuable first step is to realize you aren't "bad" or "weak" for not having been able to set boundaries up to this point. Remember, this is a learned process, one that directly contradicts the codependent patterns so many of us are taught in our early lives. It isn't too late to learn it. You can change those patterns. The effort that change requires will be repaid many times over: with less tension and more safety in your daily life, with closer relationships, and with a satisfying awareness of and respect for your own value.

Chapter Six Reflections

Any time you want to create something new or different, obstacles exist that can limit your success. To help limit the negative impact from obstacles is to recognize the obstacles and create a plan to work through them. Success in creating true boundaries requires recognizing the obstacles before and during creation of the limits, coming up with successful consequences, and consistently following through.

What obstacles hold you back from creating true boundaries?

1 = no fear obstacle   10 = totally immovable fear obstacle

Limit	Looking Bad	Hurting Others	Conflict	Change	Admitting Something is Wrong	Changing Familiar Patterns	Losing Some thing	Losing Relationship

Limit	Enjoy Negative Attention	Enjoy Control	Enjoy Victim Blame	Enjoy What Is Familiar	Loss of Negative Attention	Loss of Control	Loss of Blame, Guilt, Shame, Victim Status	Loss of Familiar

Comments or Reflections:

List the ways you were taught to set boundaries.

_____

_____

_____

List the ways you were not taught to set boundaries.

_____

_____

_____

If codependency has been involved, list the ways it has impacted your ability to set boundaries.

_____

_____

_____

List the ways you hope to change your behaviors to create successful boundaries.

_____

_____

_____

TOOLS FOR BUILDING SELF-RESPECT WITH TRUE BOUNDARIES

"Whatever you put up with is exactly what you will have."

— Anonymous

Gavin would like to create true boundaries with his young children about bedtimes, chores, and being ready for school on time. Brianna would like to create true boundaries with her sister, who shows up late every time they plan to do something together. Wyatt would like to create true boundaries with his boss, who keeps asking him to run personal errands for her during his lunch hour. Merilee would like to create true boundaries to protect herself from her abusive, alcoholic husband.

At first glance, it may seem that boundaries mean something different in each of these four circumstances. Each of these four people might appear to desire different tools or different approaches to create the boundaries appropriate to their situations.

Yet, in each case, the true boundary process can be used effectively. You can use boundaries to create safety, mutual respect, and closeness in a variety of relationships, such as:

- **People you have authority over or responsibility for:** These might include children, students, or employees.

- **Peers:** These could be spouses, friends, siblings, coworkers, and other adults in general.

- **People in positions of authority over you:** These could include employers, supervisors, parents, teachers, those in law enforcement, or other officials.

- **People who intimidate you:** Some of these, like employers, might be in positions of authority. Others may actually be peers or even those, like children, you are responsible for. They are intimidating, not necessarily because of their positions, but because the relationship is one where you perceive yourself as a victim and perceive them as better than you, more important than you, bullies, or abusers.

Each of these circumstances, on the surface, involves people in different positions of authority, age, power, or status. Each time, though, the foundation for creating boundaries is mutual respect. Healthy, respectful true boundaries are based on a recognition of your fundamental equality as human beings, which is separate from your roles or positions. One reason boundaries are effective is that they honor this equality. They encourage you to communicate respectfully, person to person, rather than as someone "higher" or "greater than" to someone "lower" or "less than." Regardless of age or status, everyone, including yourself, deserves respect as a fellow human being, and when you receive that respect from yourself, you respond with respect in turn.

Mutual respect is based on self-respect. If you don't respect yourself, you can't truly respect others, either. If you don't value yourself, you are likely to follow a codependent pattern of putting others in first place and yourself in second place or even lower. Yet habitually treating others as if they're more important than you are isn't respecting them; it's fearing, controlling, manipulating, or trying to take care of them. Even if you appear to be outwardly respectful toward them, you will be emotionally disrespectful because you can't respect others more than you respect yourself.

Learning to create true boundaries, then, requires learning to respect yourself as well as others. Some of the tools that can help build self-respect include learning to acknowledge and process your true feelings, achieving success with small boundaries, and building a support network.

Learning to Acknowledge and Process Feelings

One of the fundamental aspects of true boundaries is acting with emotional neutrality when you set limits and follow through with consequences. You cannot create boundaries successfully when you act out strong feelings such as fear, hurt, or anger. Yet to be able to reach that point of emotional neutrality, it's essential to learn to acknowledge and process your true feelings.

This lesson is necessary because most of us have learned from childhood to hide our feelings. Children are often taught that feelings like sadness, fear, and anger are "bad" while feelings like happiness and joy are "good." You learn that "bad" feelings are to be avoided or at least not expressed, while even "good" feelings should not be expressed too strongly.

This learning is not the same as consciously choosing not to express your feelings out of politeness or appropriateness. Hiding your feelings is a much deeper learning, often unconscious and done to protect yourself. You are taught to deny that you even have those feelings. Emotionally disconnecting from your true feelings in this way is telling yourself a lie that you do not matter and discounting your inner truth, which is disrespectful to yourself.

Hiding or denying your feelings, however, doesn't make them disappear. They still exist, and they have to be expressed in some fashion. When you learn not to feel and express your true feelings in direct and healthy ways, they often come out as sideways feelings, which are disrespectful of both yourself and others.

One way feelings are expressed sideways is through manipulative or passive/aggressive behavior. For example, a little boy who is angry at his older sister may have learned not to express or even consciously feel that anger, but he may "accidentally" break one of her toys.

Another way of expressing feelings sideways is by unconsciously disguising them or burying them under other feelings. Anxiety, for example, may be hiding hurt or sadness. Fear may be hidden under anger. When you are treated disrespectfully, you might respond with feelings of anger. Exploring further might show you that under the anger is a deeper level of hurt and sadness. Or an initial feeling of anger may be covering a deeper fear. Surface anxiety may hide loneliness, grief, guilt, or sadness. The feelings that emerge first are often secondary or sideways feelings that you have been taught to consider acceptable in the environment you grew up in. These feelings are also hurtful to yourself, others, things of importance, and God. The deeper level reveals the genuine feelings that are your true responses. These deeper feelings are always respectful of yourself, others, things of importance, and God. There is no formula or particular sequence for these levels of emotion; everyone's circumstances and experiences are so varied that each person is different. What matters most is to become able to accept the truth of your deeper feelings instead of continuing a pattern of pretending things are okay.

To create true boundaries, you need to learn how to recognize and acknowledge your true feelings. These core feelings are part of your most genuine self, the aspect often described as the inner child. When you connect with these true feelings and emotions, you restore your connection with the part of you that knows you are valuable and worthy of respect. This connection gives you the clarity to express your feelings in a true, straight fashion. Unlike feelings expressed sideways, which are disrespectful of yourself and others, straight feelings are respectful of yourself and others.

One emotion often tied to a pattern of disrespectful behavior is anger. In some cases, part of the energy that helps you realize you need to create boundaries may come from anger. This feeling can be one of the signals that indicates you are being treated with disrespect. It helps you come to a point of having had enough and realizing, "This isn't right; I don't deserve to be treated this way."

Yet you cannot create true boundaries out of anger, whether it is straightforward or sideways. Any limits and consequences you set out of anger are almost certainly going to be punishments, growing out of a wish to get even or take revenge. They will heighten feelings on both sides, rather than reducing feelings the way true boundaries do. You are not likely to be successful at following through with the consequences, and even if you are, the result will be more distance and tension in the relationship instead of increased closeness.

To illustrate why anger-based boundaries don't work, let's suppose Nola's teenage son, Adrian, has borrowed her car with the understanding that he is supposed to fill the gas tank before he returns it. He brings it back with the gas gauge on "empty." This is the third time this has happened, and Nola is angry about it.

If Nola has not learned to acknowledge and process her feelings, she may act out of her anger without realizing it is being expressed sideways. She might yell at Adrian, forbid him ever to borrow her car again, or punish him in some other way. She may believe she is creating a boundary, but whatever she does out of anger will be disrespectful and a punishment rather than a consequence. Her son will probably respond with anger and defensiveness. The result will be increased anger from both of them, possibly with yelling or arguing. This will increase the disrespect and conflict between them, and it won't solve the problem of Adrian's neglecting to fill the gas tank.

If Nola wants to succeed in creating a true boundary with Adrian about borrowing her car, it is necessary to process and release the anger she feels about his disrespectful behavior. If she has learned to connect with her true feelings, she will be able to reflect more deeply before she reacts. This may allow her to connect with deeper feelings such as hurt, disappointment, fear, or sadness that are the driving energy for her anger. Then she will be able to release the anger in a respectful way. Connecting with her true feelings is respectful of herself, anyone else, anything of importance, and God.

Releasing an emotion is not at all the same thing as rejecting the feeling or "letting it go." Feeling angry when you are treated with disrespect is perfectly appropriate. It isn't helpful to pretend you don't feel angry or to tell yourself you shouldn't feel angry. The goal of processing anger is not to bury it, but to accept and acknowledge it without holding on to it, and at the same time, to connect with your deeper emotional truth while respecting yourself and others, rather than letting it out sideways. The purpose is to become able to let go of that desire for revenge, since it drives the sideways anger. When you are able to get beyond the short-term wish to get even, you increase your ability to reach the larger goal of being treated with respect and becoming closer to the other person.

Many ways exist to process and/or release feelings and emotions. For relatively small incidents like the example here, one effective tool is a time-out. Take a break, perhaps for a few minutes, a few hours, or overnight. You might write in a journal, go for a drive and scream as loudly as possible with the windows up, or do something that helps connect to the emotional truth that creates a natural inner peace or emotional neutrality in the situation. When you can be more emotionally neutral, the boundary-setting process will be more effective.

More intense feelings and emotions around bigger issues may require much more processing because of the level of emotional history attached to the situation. Some tools that may be useful are:

- **Journaling:** Writing can be a way to identify and express what you are feeling. It works best to write quickly and freely, for your eyes only, writing whatever comes to mind even if it is unrelated, without stopping to edit or worrying about grammar, punctuation, or spelling. Do not critique the journaling in any fashion because any critique taps into the part of the brain that will be ineffective in creating change.

- **Scribbling:** Scribbling is somewhat like journaling without words. Just scribbling freely on a page, without drawing or writing anything specific, can help you release energy and connect with your feelings. This technique works best with a clipboard and a sturdy ball-point pen. Scribble in a back-and-forth motion as fast and hard as you can. If the paper rips, get another sheet. This technique works best with great intensity and continuing until the energy is dissipated. In some situations, you can use up a number of sheets of paper and take well over five minutes.

- **Physical expression:** Beating on a mattress or pillow, without breaking things or harming yourself or anyone else, can be a way to release energy and work through feelings. It can be especially useful with anger as a way to explore more deeply and access the grief or sadness that may lie beneath that anger. This process often ends with tears—a sign it's working well to help you get past anger that has blocked your ability to grieve. Sometimes the level and intensity of anger generates a desire to create loud noise and destroy something to feel the anger's full intensity. Some clients have found beating on a large drum or trash can as fast and hard as they can has helped create the desired emotional release.

• **Screaming without words:** Screaming without words is another effective way to help access deeper feelings. Like beating on a mattress, it can often help you get past feelings of anger and hurt and reach a point of healing tears and grieving. Screaming without words is actually a natural way you are designed to release some of this energy.

While these tools can be used by yourself, processing deep feelings often works best with a counselor. *Finding Emotional Freedom* includes more information on finding counselors, counseling methods, and the process of recovery. For anyone who has been affected by addiction, abuse, or other kinds of emotional trauma, counseling can be a valuable and even necessary tool. It can be the starting point for building enough self-respect to create and follow through with true boundaries.

Practice and Small Successes

While self-respect is essential for creating true boundaries, building self-respect doesn't always have to be the first step in the process. In many cases, learning to create true boundaries can actually be a tool for building self-respect.

The key is to start small. By starting with minor boundaries, where the stakes are smaller, you increase your chances of being successful in following through. These small successes help to build your confidence and increase the respect you have for yourself. Starting with small boundaries and creating successes around boundary-setting can be equally beneficial for the person you are setting the boundaries with because they also are able to see and feel the success. This success makes it possible for them to also start trusting the boundary-setting process at some level and to see that your follow-through, which creates the safety and respect, will be there.

Succeeding with small boundaries makes it easier to create larger boundaries around more significant and emotionally charged issues. Gradually building your boundary-creating skills in this way fosters increasing awareness of your own value and gives you even more strength to follow through with consequences when others treat you disrespectfully.

As discussed in the previous chapter, fear is one of the obstacles that makes it difficult to follow through with true boundaries. Your fears of conflict, upsetting others, and being the "bad guy" most often surface during the testing phase of creating boundaries. When you start with small boundaries, the process of testing gives you a chance to practice walking through minor conflict. When you do so successfully, you learn you can do it, which helps you try again and succeed again. As well as building confidence, this repeated practice in doing what is unfamiliar also helps rewire the brain so you are no longer stuck in the same old patterns you have learned. This rewiring is what creates long-term healthy behavioral change, which is the ultimate goal.

Starting with minor issues can also help overcome another obstacle: lack of energy. One response I sometimes hear from clients when faced with the idea of creating true boundaries is, "I'm so overwhelmed I don't have the energy for it." This lack of energy is most often genuine. Not having true boundaries, but instead trying to emotionally take care of everyone except yourself, can be emotionally exhausting. Living with anger and resentment, and repressing the emotional energy associated with your true feelings, also drains a lot of energy. Ironically, living without true boundaries uses up and wastes much more energy than it takes to create and maintain true boundaries.

Initially, the idea of creating some level of change with boundaries can seem overwhelming because you are used to expending a certain amount of energy in your daily living with no boundaries. Creating true boundaries seems to be one more task, responsibility, or energy drain to consume the little bit of energy you have left. In the beginning, some energy is required to get others to realize you will be responding differently. Changing existing patterns does take a certain amount of energy, though typically less energy than it takes to live without true boundaries. Once others accept the reality that you will consistently follow through, the resistance becomes much less and the compliance increases.

Still, in the beginning, you may not have the energy to tackle boundaries around a large issue. Stacy, for example, might feel overwhelmed at the idea of setting a limit with her alcoholic husband by telling him she will no longer call his boss with excuses if he is too hungover to go to work. But she may be able to create a boundary at work with a coworker who borrows her supplies without asking permission. Success with the smaller issue can show her that true boundaries help build energy.

Another important reason for starting small with boundaries is perfectionism. Many of us have been taught to believe that we have to do something perfectly. If we can't, we might as well give up. Yet there's no way, when you're just learning a new skill, that you can do it perfectly. If you're just beginning to learn the cello, of course, you can't play like Yo-Yo Ma. Believing you should be able to play that well is disrespectful to him and to yourself because it ignores both his talent and the many hours of practice that have developed his skill—hours you have not yet invested.

Learning to create boundaries is really no different from learning any other skill. Since it is new, of course you'll make mistakes. Of course you'll need to practice. That's why it's so important to start with minor issues. When the stakes are small, it's easier to back up and try again. It is also easier to tackle larger issues when the smaller boundary successes have already taken place. When you begin with small boundaries, it's much easier to see those that don't succeed as practice and understand them as learning opportunities rather than failures. If you set a small limit or consequence that turns out to be inappropriate, you can learn from that experience and start over or modify the boundary to be more appropriate. If you fail to follow through with a consequence, you can figure out why so you can create a consequence you can follow through with next time. It also helps to remember that if you try to create a boundary and fail, you haven't made things worse. After all, you didn't have a boundary in place before. You are still in the same position, which means you are free to start over.

Yet one more reason for starting with small boundaries is what people in Twelve-Step programs sometimes call "fake it till you make it." Creating boundaries in small ways can help you change the behavior that shows other people you don't respect yourself. When you don't believe you are worthy of respect, your behavior and body language reflect that belief and communicate to other people that you don't value yourself. In response, they tend not to value you either. This makes it more likely—even if they love and care about you—that they will bully, disregard, and run over you. Acting as if you deserve respect, even when you aren't sure you believe you do, can begin to teach yourself and others to treat you with respect.

This outward behavior isn't enough by itself because your body language will still show you don't truly value yourself. Yet it's a start and can be a useful part of the process of building genuine self-respect.

In addition to starting small, it's important to follow the specific process set out in Chapters Two, Three, and Four. This process gives you a guide to follow, even if you think you can't do it or even if you are afraid. The details of the process, like writing out the limits and the positive and negative consequences, do matter. They help you connect, both emotionally and spiritually, with your own true self as well as with the other person. The process is a structure that works; it is something you can trust even if you don't believe you can trust yourself. Trusting and respecting the process can help you learn to trust and respect yourself.

For someone living in chaos, conflict, and even fear, it may seem trivial to create boundaries about leaving dirty dishes in the living room or feeding the cat. Yet small boundaries hold a lot of power. They are the threads that, consistently used, eventually create strong new patterns of safety, respect, and closeness. In helping clients learn to create boundaries, I have seen this truth in action many times.

After nearly fifteen years of marriage, Krista and Stewart's relationship was filled with rage and emotional abuse, which was escalating toward physical abuse. Krista was afraid of her husband, and she was equally afraid of ending the relationship because she believed, with good reason, that he would harm her if she tried to leave. Learning to create small boundaries was a major part of reducing her fear. One little boundary at a time, Krista began to show her newfound respect for herself. Stewart responded by learning to respect her as well. One small success led to another and then another, and slowly, the boundaries grew bigger. Stewart was more willing to comply with larger boundaries around his abusive behavior because a habit of compliance had been built with the smaller boundaries.

Those little boundaries that Krista began with gradually formed a strong and safe pathway of power and recovery. While Krista's original intent in setting the boundaries was to create safety and not have the marriage end in divorce, the mutual respect the boundaries created allowed both spouses to see how the relationship limited their self-respect and growth.

A Network of Support

Disrespectful patterns of thinking and behavior that teach you that you don't deserve true boundaries do not develop in isolation. They are taught to you, most often in childhood, by your emotional history, environment, and the people around you, even if that was not the intention. Since you learn those patterns through your interactions with others, it's often easier to change them when you have the help of others. As you are learning to create true boundaries, it is helpful to form a network of mutual support.

Support people in your life are able to listen objectively without interjecting their unsolicited opinions or their own need to fix. They listen when you share, and you listen when they share. These are people you are able to share your emotional truth with and know they will continue to be your friends and supporters. Usually, your support network is most fruitful without family members because typically family members have a vested interest that limits their ability to be open and objective.

A typical support network may have as few as three or as many as six people you connect with at least weekly. If the sharing in the relationship becomes lopsided, it is not a mutually supportive relationship, and it, ultimately, may no longer be effective in supporting both parties.

A network of supportive people can help foster your awareness of your own value in several ways.

- **Learning about true boundaries:** Spending time with others— friends, family members, colleagues, or counselors—who model healthy behavior around true boundaries can help you learn how to do the same. This can give you a platform to inquire, observe, practice, and even role-play the boundaries you wish to set.

- **Getting a different perspective:** Supportive people can share their experiences of what has and has not worked for them. Someone who listens, without giving advice, allows you to vent, process, reflect, and come up with new options.

- **Processing feelings and emotions:** Counselors, Twelve-Step groups, workshops, and therapy groups can be safe and supportive places to learn to be heard as you identify, express, feel, and release your feelings and emotions. Friends and family members who are able to listen and be supportive without judging or giving advice can also be helpful.

- **Creating limits and consequences:** Discussing true boundaries with a neutral third party can often help you make sure the limits and consequences you create are appropriate.

- **Helping you change negative self-talk:** When you don't believe you have the right to set limits, or you don't believe others will respect your limits, it is easy to talk yourself out of creating a true boundary even before you try. The codependent patterns you may have learned are maintained by negative self-talk.

  Here are examples of the negative things you may tell yourself about creating boundaries:

  - "It's a waste of time."
  - "It's stupid."

- "Nobody will listen to me anyway."
- "It's not a big deal."
- "It's too much work."
- "It's too scary."
- "I might get hurt."
- "Nice people don't do that."
- "I shouldn't have to say it; if they loved me, they'd know."
- "I shouldn't have to set any boundaries."
- "It doesn't matter what I do."
- "Nobody cares anyway."

All these negative messages that you repeat inside your own head are based on a learned expectation that you only matter when someone else notices or takes care of you and the criticism that you take on. To work through and release the negative messages requires you to explore the unresolved feelings and emotions associated with the negative message, and to release those feelings with the support and encouragement of another safe person. When the unresolved feelings and emotions are released, the need for the negative message no longer exists and your self-worth increases. The increase of self-worth makes it much easier to set and follow through with true boundaries.

- **Encouraging you to focus on successes:** It isn't easy to change old patterns that tell you that you are not worthy of respect, so it's important to have others provide you with support and encouragement. Sometimes it helps just to be able to talk with someone and say, "This is hard." It's even better, though, if that person can remind you of your successes. What is even more valuable is when you can honestly and sincerely recognize your successes. You may tend to focus on negatives and on your mistakes, in part, because that's what is familiar.

When you're in the process of changing your behavior, it's also hard to see your own progress. For example, I once worked with an overweight client who was sure she was not doing well at staying within the daily calorie limits she had established. I suggested creating a chart to track the meals and snacks she ate. At the end of a week, she had a chart with forty-two entries (six meals and snacks each day). Of those forty-two entries, how many times had she failed to stay within her limits? Two. That's a significant success rate by any standard. Yet, because she focused on those two failures, she still felt she wasn't succeeding. It was helpful to have her reframe her success so she could start to shift her focus.

§§§§§

If you are like most people, you have been taught to wait to receive respect from others instead of respecting yourself. You have learned a codependent pattern that goes like this: "I'm taking care of you because I see you as important and myself as not important, so I think, in turn, you should take care of me." That unspoken expectation is a "string" attached to the belief that you don't matter. Another part of the pattern is that your expectation of getting cared for in return is rarely met. This is the source of the resentment that is such an integral part of codependency and lack of self-respect.

This pattern is not deliberate. You don't consciously choose not to respect or value yourself. Instead, you learn that belief at such a deep, unconscious level that typically you don't even realize it is there.

When you become able to recognize this hidden pattern, you

can start making conscious choices to act in ways that support your sense of self-respect. One choice you can make is to learn to create true boundaries.

Becoming aware of your own worth is vital to overcoming the fears and codependent patterns that keep you from setting limits with those around you. The foundation of true boundaries is accepting a truth many of us were never taught: You are a worthwhile, precious individual who deserves to feel your true feelings and have safety, respect, and closeness in your life and relationships. Learning to create mutual respect through boundaries takes you back to the sense of self-worth that is your birthright. Boundaries give you emotional wings.

Chapter Seven Reflections

When asked, most people initially believe that they respect themselves. When they are invited to explore different patterns in their lives, they may see they have little self-respect. Many believe that if they take care of and respect others, they are respecting themselves, yet they may actually be disrespecting themselves.

To truly respect yourself means that you are aware of, connect with, and express your true feelings in a respectful way to validate and release them.

In what ways do you give yourself self-respect that does not involve another person?

_____

_____

_____

List the ways you become aware of your true feelings.

_____

_____

List the ways you give yourself permission to feel and express your feelings in a respectful fashion.

_____

_____

_____

List the feelings that are limiting your ability to set and follow through with true feelings.

_____

_____

_____

1 = no effect   10 = totally effective

Tools	Effective Emotional Connection	Specific Technique	Comments
Journaling			
Scribbling			
Physical Expression			
Screaming Without Words			

Comments or Reflections:

_____

_____

_____

Go back to the written boundaries in Chapter 3's Reflections and prioritize the easiest to the most difficult on the basis of self-respect.

_____

_____

_____

Of the boundaries set, which ones are demonstrating respect and which ones require modifications?

_____

_____

List your support network.

_____

_____

_____

Which support people will be most helpful in the modification process of the boundaries set?

_____

_____

_____

TEACHING THROUGH TRUE BOUNDARIES

"You best teach others about healthy boundaries by enforcing yours."

— Bryant McGill

When you consistently practice the skill of creating boundaries, you become more comfortable with them. You gradually replace old patterns of disrespect, guilt, shame, and codependency with new patterns of respect for yourself and others. Eventually, showing mutual respect with healthy true boundaries becomes a habit—a behavior that is familiar and normal.

One benefit of living with true boundaries is what it teaches you and those around you. When you model mutually respectful behavior, you give others the opportunity to learn to do the same. That teaching applies to you and to everyone else in your life, whether they are children, subordinates, peers, or authority figures.

True Boundaries Teach Others How to Treat You

Creating true boundaries is a learned skill. Especially if you were taught codependent patterns based on fear, manipulation, and lack of respect, learning a different way of interacting with the people in your life can be challenging. Not only do you need to learn new, more respectful patterns for yourself; you need to teach those patterns to those around you who also have learned and practiced the old ones.

What adds to the difficulty is that, just because you reach a point of respecting yourself and being ready to change old patterns of behavior, the people in your life don't automatically get to that change point with you. In fact, most of the time, they are probably not ready to change. This means they probably won't be enthusiastic about your changing, either. Because a relationship changes when one person in the relationship changes, it's common for the other person to resist the change. This resistance often results in a period of increased conflict, at first, as others test your boundaries.

The key to dealing with this conflict is following through, consistently and neutrally, with both positive and negative consequences. When you follow through, time after time after time, others will eventually learn to respect your boundaries. While you can't control other people's behavior or force them to change, you can teach them how to treat you in new and more respectful ways.

Just one caveat here: Increasing safety and mutual respect in a relationship with boundaries does not mean ending conflict in the relationship. One person disagreeing with another or expressing anger in a straight and authentic way is not disrespectful. Straight anger is respectful of oneself, others, God, and things; it does not do anything to create regret. It is sideways anger, which comes out abusively or manipulatively, that is disrespectful. Following through with boundaries is one way to teach the people in your life how to express anger in straight and respectful ways.

True boundaries do not try to squash, manipulate, or set limits on other people's feelings. You can, however, create boundaries about the way others express those feelings to you. A limit such as, "If your anger is straight and respectful, I will listen. If you show disrespect when you get angry, the conversation is over," focuses on the other person's feelings in a way that is not respectful or useful. A limit such as, "Name calling is no longer going to be allowed," addresses the other person's disrespectful behavior rather than the feelings.

True Boundaries Teach Children Mutual Respect

Creating consistent true boundaries with children helps reduce conflict, foster safety, and build respect. The short-term benefit is a calmer, more comfortable family life for everyone. The long-term benefit, however, matters even more. When children grow up with true boundaries, they learn valuable life lessons. When they are allowed to experience the positive and negative consequences of their actions, they learn there are always consequences for the things they do and the choices they make, and they learn to take responsibility for their choices. When they are treated with respect, they learn to act with respect toward others. When they see parents acting with respect for themselves, they learn to do the same.

Here are some ways to teach children about true boundaries:

A. **Model true boundaries, both directly with your children and also with other people in your life.**

Respectful boundaries, just like any other behavior, are taught most effectively by example. Our children learn what they see us do. It is ineffective, for example, if an angry and frustrated parent tells a child, "You have to respect me because I'm your parent." Such a statement won't generate respect because it does not demonstrate respect. When parents teach one thing by their words and the opposite by their actions, children respond with defiance or with compliance but not respect. When parents use punishments instead of limits and consequences, children will find ways to punish, manipulate, or hurt parents in turn—even if their reaction hurts themselves, as well.

Larry's daughter Erin, an eighth-grader, does her homework faithfully but is careless about taking it to school. Larry has fallen into a pattern of nagging and reminding her, as well as making trips to school to deliver the homework when she forgets it. Eventually, he tells Erin he will no longer remind her or take forgotten homework to school for her. If she remembers it, she will receive credit for turning in the assignment. If she forgets it, she will get a zero or whatever other consequence the teacher imposes.

Two days later, Erin calls her father from school: She forgot to put her English paper into her backpack, and if she doesn't turn it in, she will get a zero on a major assignment.

If Larry follows through with the boundary, he will politely and neutrally refuse to take the assignment to school and will respectfully end the conversation. He will not punish Erin, scold her, or even talk about the missed homework. Erin will experience the negative consequence of getting a failing grade on that homework assignment, which will help her learn to be responsible for her own actions. She will also learn that her father can be trusted to keep his word.

If Larry makes an exception and takes the homework to school, "just this once," because the assignment is important, he will erase the boundary. This exception will teach Erin that she doesn't need to take responsibility for herself. She will also learn that her father can't be relied on to mean what he says.

Zoe is the office manager for a small real estate firm, where her schedule is supposed to be limited to regular Monday-through-Friday office hours. Yet her boss often calls her on evenings or weekends, expecting Zoe to be available to answer accounting questions or come into the office to solve problems like unjamming the printer. Zoe doesn't get paid for this extra work. She resents the demands, especially when they interrupt family activities like her son Carson's soccer games. She complains to her family, but she doesn't do anything to set limits with her boss.

By tolerating her boss's disrespectful behavior, Zoe is teaching Carson several problematic lessons. Some of the beliefs he might learn from her lack of boundaries are: employees are powerless victims, Carson is not as important as work, work is more important than family time, and being taken advantage of by employers is acceptable.

B. Respect children's inherent boundaries and treat them with respect.

The fundamental truth underlying boundaries is the awareness that, regardless of our age or status, each of us is entitled to be respected as a unique and valuable human being. For parents to receive respect from their children, it's essential to give respect to them, beginning when they are babies. Even very young children can communicate messages about boundaries with both words and body language.

When Susanna walked into her daughter's house, her nine-month-old grandson, Henry, came crawling over. Obviously happy to see her, he sat up and gave her a big grin. Susanna squatted and held out her hands, offering to pick him up. Instead of reaching up toward her, Henry put his hands down, communicating quite clearly that he did not want to be held. Respecting his wish, Susanna left him to play while she sat down to talk with his mother. A short time later, Henry came over and pulled himself up to stand beside Susanna's chair. This time when she offered to pick him up, he responded eagerly, ready to sit on her lap and snuggle.

Three-year-old Brienne was sitting on a little chair beside her grandfather, who was visiting. He reached down to stroke her hair, and then he began tickling her. She told him, "Don't touch me." His response was, "But I love you. I'm your grandpa, so I can do that." Brienne got up, took her chair, and went over to sit beside her father to create her own safety and respect.

Parents are told to teach children about "bad touch" to protect them against abuse. One of the strongest forms of protection is to teach them, by example, what "good touch" is. This includes letting kids be in charge of their bodies from an early age. Washing them, changing diapers, changing clothes, and other types of care can be done with respect; not by force, but with the child's cooperation and permission. This doesn't necessarily mean allowing toddlers to decide whether they need baths or whether diapers need to be changed. It is more a matter of taking care of their bodies in a matter-of-fact, respectful, and emotionally neutral way. Respectful touch also means starting early to encourage them to help and take responsibility for themselves in ways such as washing themselves in the bathtub.

Respecting children's bodies and respecting their right to say "no" helps create an environment of safety and trust. Children treated with this kind of respect are more likely to feel safe enough to tell parents if they do encounter "bad touch."

When adults pick up, kiss, tickle, or otherwise touch babies and toddlers, without allowing the child a choice or waiting for permission, most often their intent is loving. Even so, the message the children receive is, "I don't have the right to say who can and who cannot touch my body," which is a form of disrespect.

Children of any age who are neglected, yelled at, called names, hit, or sexually abused also receive the same message of disrespect, but in a much more traumatic and destructive way. For these children, the message "You are not worthy of respect" is deeper and causes much more lasting harm. The belief that they have no right to set boundaries or be treated with respect can be very difficult to overcome.

A more subtle form of disrespect with older children often takes the form of stereotyping and negative expectations. Just think, for example, of all the eye-rolling comments parents share about "the way teenagers are." When you expect them to be irresponsible, disrespectful, or rebellious, you are teaching them to behave that way.

The emotionally neutral component of following through with consequences is especially helpful with children because it helps create a safe environment where they learn they can trust parents and tell the truth. For example, suppose Nick, who is seventeen, has just dropped off his girlfriend at 11:45 on a Saturday night and is on his way home when he has a flat tire. His curfew is midnight, and he's not going to make it home on time. He calls his parents to explain why he'll be late.

In this case, Nick is not complying with the limit of "You need to be home by midnight." Yet by calling his parents, he is being respectful and honoring the boundary. The boundary's underlying goal, to create safety and closeness, is being met. If the parents believe Nick's explanation and help him get home safely, perhaps by making sure he can change the tire or by offering to come get him, they show they respect and trust him. This teaches him it's safe to tell them the truth. When parents create a pattern of trust in this way, they help create safety even in more serious situations. If Nick or someone he is in a car with has been drinking, for example, he will be more likely to call and ask his parents to come get him—an action that could save his life.

C. Start small.

Just as starting small is important in learning to create boundaries, it is also important in teaching children about boundaries.

Obviously, different limits and consequences are needed for children of different ages, abilities, and needs. Yet following through fairly and consistently with boundaries for all the children in a family meets the larger goal of creating safety and respect. It doesn't matter that an eight- and a fifteen-year-old have different bedtimes; what matters is that they both have bedtimes. When you set appropriate limits and follow through with consequences, you establish a pattern of mutual respect and responsibility. True boundaries become the norm and a way of life. Children learn from an early age that parents are serious about limits and consequences, so peace and respect are fostered even as the children get older.

Managing allowances is one example of boundaries evolving as children get older. Suppose Gabe is eight and his sister Arianna is fourteen. His weekly allowance is $3.00 and hers is $15.00. Yet their parents have set three important limits about allowances that apply to both children: First, their assigned chores and responsibilities are to be completed. Second, they are required to save 10 percent. Third, their allowance is meant to last through the week. Once they spend it, their parents will not give or loan them more money.

Encouraging children to make age-appropriate choices and listening to their ideas and opinions also teach them mutual respect. This does not mean having children make decisions that are the parents' responsibility; it means allowing them input while being clear that parents have the final say.

Allowing children to make decisions that should be reserved for adults is disrespectful in several ways. It teaches children to be entitled instead of being responsible. It gives them power they have not learned how to use, so naturally they are likely to misuse it. Then parents may criticize, blame, and shame the child. This kind of enmeshment, which puts the children in the parents' place, is confusing for children and teaches them insecurity and disrespect.

As an example, suppose Gabe and Arianna's mother takes them shopping for winter coats. She might encourage Gabe to make a choice such as, "Do you want the red coat or the blue one?" She doesn't allow him to make larger decisions like how much to spend or whether he needs a new coat. Within similar limits, she might give Arianna more options: "I will spend fifty dollars on a coat. You can choose from these that are on sale. If you want the expensive brand name coat instead, you need to pay the difference."

D. Support children in creating true boundaries with other people, both within and outside of the family.

    1. Bullying among siblings

        A typical boundary that may be created at home concerns bullying or picking on a sibling. The ideal, of course, would be for parents to establish such true boundaries from the time a second child is born. Since this doesn't typically happen, many siblings develop patterns of picking on one another. Once these patterns have been established, creating true boundaries around bullying is more of a challenge, but it still can be done successfully.

        Suppose, for example, that Tanya is thirteen and her brother Eli is nine. She routinely calls him disrespectful names, yells at him, and makes fun of him and his friends. She throws a fit if he goes into her room or touches any of her belongings, but she doesn't hesitate to use anything of his that she wants. If it's Tanya's turn to clean the family room and any of Eli's toys have been left there, she simply throws them away. Even when she's being nice to her little brother, she often has an agenda, such as manipulating him into doing her chores.

Here are two boundaries the parents might establish:

- **Name-calling:** Tanya is given the limit that name-calling and yelling are not acceptable. As long as that limit is respected, the positive consequence is that life goes on as usual. If the limit is not respected, Eli is given specific permission to shout "Stop! No name-calling!" He is also given permission and expected to tell the parents. If any of Eli's friends are made fun of or called names, they are also expected to tell Eli's parents. Tanya's consequence for failing to respect the limit on name-calling is to write a sincere letter of apology to her brother and to each person she has offended, including herself, and to read each letter to Eli and each of Eli's friends she has offended in the presence of one or both parents.

- **Failing to respect Eli's space and belongings:** The limit is that no one goes into other family members' bedrooms, uses their belongings, or disposes of their belongings without permission. An appropriate positive consequence is that life goes on as usual. An appropriate negative consequence for violating this limit is a time-out of perhaps fifteen minutes, during which that person is encouraged to reflect on how they would feel if someone invaded their space or used their things. At the end of the time-out, a formal written apology would be given. If Tanya throws away or damages Eli's belongings, buying replacements with her own money would be an appropriate consequence. Again, the positive consequence for respecting the limit is that life goes on as usual.

In creating true boundaries around bullying at home, it's

helpful to keep the following elements in mind:

a. It can be beneficial when negative consequences focus on encouraging reflection. A formal written apology to the person they have bullied and another to themselves does this, which is one reason it is so often an appropriate consequence in conflict between siblings. Writing the apology also takes enough time and effort that a child won't want to do it, but not so much time that it is a punishment. Most parents' response to a bullying situation is to take away all screens for an extended period of time. Since screens usually do not relate to the bullying, it is a punishing and bullying response, which validates the bullying behavior. The time for reflection and the writing of the apology directly relate to the bullying, and the screens are not used because they are a distraction rather than a way to bully in return. When someone chooses to bully another person, they are also choosing not to use their screens or be involved in other activities. When the reflection and apology are completed, access to the screens and other activities continue as normal.

b. Since the purpose of true boundaries is to increase safety and closeness, one component of boundaries around bullying is to create an environment where it is safe for children to tell the truth. This may include giving children specific permission to tell parents about bullying, and to not dismiss or discount what they say. At times, however, kids may seek revenge by lying or exaggerating, so consequences for lying about being bullied may be necessary as well. The goal is to provide an environment where all the children in the family can trust their parents to believe them, take them seriously, and support them.

c. One reason bullying between siblings is difficult to deal with is it often takes place behind the parents' backs. In creating boundaries, then, it's important to frame consequences that help change the behavior by bringing it into the open. It can be effective to establish limits and consequences that encourage kids to bring more of their interactions into the parents' presence. Requiring children to do homework in the living room rather than in their rooms may be an appropriate consequence. If bullying takes place when older kids are babysitting younger ones, an appropriate consequence may be to hire a sitter for all of them the following day.

d. Positive attention for both children who act like bullies and those who are bullied is important in changing a pattern of bullying. This is one reason for negative consequences that help bring behavior into the open and discourage kids' isolation. It can also be helpful to increase family time in ways that are framed as positive attention rather than consequences: parents and children playing games together, taking a walk together, riding bikes, or having conversations, for example.

Just as with other boundaries, the key to changing the disrespectful pattern is setting clear limits and following through consistently with consequences. By doing so, the parents show that they can be trusted to build a family culture of respect and safety. This helps children—both those who have learned to act like bullies and those who have been picked on—to learn new, more respectful ways to interact. This teaching is important because bullies were bullied before they became a bully.

2. *Bullying at school*

If children are bullied at school, your support as the parent is important to help teach the children they are valuable and don't deserve to be treated disrespectfully. Notifying the parents and the school principal of the bully is an appropriate action. It is especially effective when the parents and principal work with the child who has been bullied to set out clear limits and positive and negative consequences. Formal written apologies associated with the bullying that are read in the presence of all parties involved is almost always an appropriate first consequence. Your role as the parent is also to support the child in following through with consequences as well as exploring ways to ensure the bullying stops.

3. *Bad touch*

Telling children not to let people touch them in bad ways is limited in its usefulness unless parents also teach children what they can do in various circumstances. For example, a parent could help children establish a real boundary by teaching them to say, "If you touch me like that, I'm going to scream." At least it becomes a real boundary if the parent also teaches the child to scream by actually practicing it. It may be important to practice the screaming without giving a warning, as well, to teach the child to do this if an unsafe touch occurs inappropriately and unexpectedly. It's also essential, just as in the example above of Nick and his curfew, that children learn the parent will listen to them, believe them, and help.

4. *True boundaries with authority figures*

Sometimes children may want to create a true boundary and believe they cannot do so because of the other person's position or role. Suppose, for example, that Miranda, a high school sophomore who struggles with math, has an algebra teacher who shames and ridicules her instead of helping her learn. Miranda knows this is wrong and disrespectful, but she is afraid that if she confronts or stands up to the teacher directly, she will only make the situation worse.

In such a situation, involvement and support from parents is crucial. Miranda's parents might encourage and help her to write a detailed description of what she is experiencing, along with the behavior changes she needs to have from the teacher. Here is a sample letter:

Dear Mrs. Jones:

When I ask questions in your class, instead of explaining, you often respond with statements like, "The rest of the class doesn't seem to have any problem." When I have asked to meet with you after school for extra help, you've told me you don't have time and I just need to work harder. Last week, you announced to the whole class that I had received the lowest grade on the weekly quiz, and from the tone of your voice, you almost seemed pleased that I hadn't done well.

This behavior does not help me learn. It also makes me feel unsafe. I have a right to be treated respectfully, without shame or ridicule. This is not the way I am being treated in your class.

From now on, I expect to be treated with respect in your class. As long as I'm treated respectfully in your class, I'll continue to work hard and actively participate. If I'm shamed, ridiculed, or treated disrespectfully in any fashion,

I will document that behavior and ask for a meeting with you, my parents, and the principal to help resolve this situation.

My intention with this boundary is to treat both of us with respect.

Sincerely,

Miranda

While support and help from her parents in writing this letter would be very helpful, only Miranda should sign it. The content makes clear that her parents and the principal will become involved if the teacher's behavior does not change. If the teacher does not begin to treat Miranda more respectfully, then a copy of the letter goes to the principal along with a request for the principal to meet with Miranda, her parents, and the teacher. The meeting's aim would not be to punish the teacher, but to get her attention in a way that will foster more respect for everyone involved.

E. *Work together as parents, and enlist support from other significant adults in children's lives*

Ideally, in creating boundaries with children, parents will discuss the limits and consequences they wish to establish, write them out together ahead of time, and then support each other in communicating the boundaries and following through. In reality, though, this doesn't always happen. One parent may be ready to change a pattern of codependency and caretaking by creating boundaries, and the other may not. Especially if parents are divorced, anger and unresolved issues between the two of them may get in the way of working together as parents.

When establishing boundaries in blended families, it is important that both parents discuss and agree on what boundaries and consequences will be established, prior to discussing them with the children. They will also work together in writing out the limits and consequences. Then it is important in blended families that the biological parent presents the boundaries and consequences with the stepparent present. This shows that the biological parent is establishing the boundaries and consequences, while the stepparent is aware of the boundaries and consequences and is given permission to follow through with the positive and negative consequences. The agreement between parents helps limit the children from trying to manipulate or divide the parents.

Creating boundaries without the support of the other parent is difficult, especially if parents are in the same house and one parent is unwilling to enforce boundaries. The parent who wants change can still establish boundaries in areas that involve the individual relationship between that parent and the child: an example might be "No borrowing my clothes without permission." This limit with appropriate consequences would begin to teach the child about boundaries. In a situation where one parent is unwilling to follow through with boundaries, the other parent may need to create boundaries with that parent as well as with the children.

If the parents are divorced, one parent can establish boundaries to create safety and respect in his or her home. Then the parent can coach the children about the rules being different in the different houses. In most cases, children already understand this, so the response of "We don't do it that way at Mom's house" is just one of the various ways they will test the boundaries.

One factor that makes creating true boundaries without the support of the other parent so challenging is that the one creating boundaries will be seen as the "bad" or "mean" parent. The most effective response to this is not to give up on true boundaries, and to follow through consistently, neutrally, and respectfully. Since true boundaries create safety and closeness, eventually children will learn to appreciate the respect they receive.

For a time, I worked with teenagers in a juvenile detention facility. When we explored true boundaries, many of them told me they wished their parents had set true boundaries for them because it would have been a sign that they mattered to their parents. Children feel loved when parents care enough to create boundaries; they understand that boundaries create a healthier, safer environment. As I have seen in my own experience and with clients, in the long term, children often become closer to the parent who creates and follows through with respectful boundaries.

In addition to working together as parents, it may be helpful in some situations to enlist support from other adults such as grandparents, day care providers, teachers, or coaches. Suppose Desiree's parents have set a limit of "No driving with more than one friend in the car." It's certainly reasonable, in the interests of Desiree's safety, to ask her grandparents to observe that same limit with her.

At the same time, it isn't respectful or realistic to expect other people who deal with your children to follow through with all of the boundaries you create as parents. In serious matters like driving or alcohol use, it may be necessary to create boundaries with other adults who don't respect limits you have set. In other areas, though, it's more useful to keep in mind that kids are smart enough to understand they may encounter different limits in different relationships or circumstances. Your role is to keep following through with your own boundaries, not to try to control or manipulate the boundaries (or lack of them) of other people in your children's lives.

F. *Recognize that boundaries teach children valuable life skills*

Setting limits and following through with consequences helps teach children to take care of themselves physically, emotionally, and practically.

Suppose Austin, at age thirteen, has been told by his parents that from now on he is responsible for doing his own laundry. He doesn't get around to it one week, which means he discovers on Sunday evening that he has no clean jeans to wear to school the next day. By allowing Austin to experience the consequences of his choice not to wash his clothes, his parents are teaching him to take responsibility for himself. By insisting that he do his own laundry, they are also teaching him a useful and practical life skill.

If children stay up past bedtime, a consequence of having an earlier bedtime the next night is another way of teaching them to take care of themselves. Going to bed earlier because you stayed up late the night before and are tired isn't a punishment. It's a sensible and supportive consequence that teaches self-care, self-respect, and discipline.

§§§§§

When you create clear and true boundaries, you teach the people in your life that both you and they are entitled to respect. You teach others, especially your children, to make decisions and live with the consequences, to accept responsibility, and to respect themselves and others. Living with true boundaries reduces conflict. It shows, by powerful example, how much more people can enjoy each other's company when they respect each other.

When you make true boundaries a part of your interactions with children from the time they are little, you teach them to be successful. You build a pattern of respect and responsibility that will serve them well for the rest of their lives.

Chapter Eight Reflections

As parents, it is our responsibility to create and set true boundaries for our children. It is the children's responsibility to validate that the boundaries actually exist by challenging them until they see that the true boundary does actually exist. Until the true boundary is established and tested to verify that it actually exists, tension in the family, with siblings, in school, and in other relationships may exist.

Many times people will ask: "Why do I have to create limits and follow through with the positive or negative consequences?" The reason is you are feeling the tension and lack of safety and respect to the point you want it to change. By creating and following through with true boundaries, you are teaching others ways they can also start to create more safety and respect in their lives.

The teaching can be about creating safety and respect by having a voice and by learning life skills, communication skills, and new ways to work as a team.

List any positive teaching you hope to create with boundaries.

_____

_____

_____

If in a relationship with children, list the boundaries you have created as a team with your partner for the children.

_____

_____

_____

If your partner is unwilling to participate in the creation of true boundaries for the children, list the boundaries you might want to create for your partner.

_____

_____

_____

List the boundaries you have implemented or are intending to implement.

_____

_____

_____

Which of the boundaries listed above have been successfully tested?

_____

_____

_____

List any boundaries that were tested and the consequences that were not followed through with.

_____

_____

_____

List what changes will help create consistent follow-through for the boundaries that did not have follow-through.

_____

_____

_____

SHOWING LOVE WITH TRUE BOUNDARIES

"Individuals set boundaries to feel safe, respected, and heard."

— Pamela Cummins

"That's so harsh." "It's so cold." "How can you be so mean?" Responses like these to true boundaries are often based on two misperceptions. One is that true boundaries are about keeping people at a distance. Many of us have been taught that boundaries are meant either as punishments or ways to control others. When you come to understand true boundaries as tools to create safety, bring people closer, and foster more respectful relationships, you can see that true boundaries are about love.

This brings us to the second misperception: Love means never having to say no.

In many cases, the failure to create boundaries with the people in our lives is based on love. However, it may be a sideways kind of love, rooted in codependency and fear, where love is confused with niceness, caretaking, or avoiding conflict, which actually creates more conflict.

This sideways or incomplete love is often involved when parents don't set clear limits or follow through with consequences for their children. The behavior can grow out of a loving desire to give children what they want. Yet in the long run, the more loving behavior is to create boundaries that give children what they need—safety, life skills, and respect for themselves and others. By way of analogy, as parents you wouldn't allow toddlers to touch a hot stove or play with sharp knives just because they wanted to; instead, you would set limits out of love and concern to keep them safe.

The kind of love inherent in true boundaries takes this larger perspective. When you create respectful boundaries, you are expressing a love that respects and wants the best for both yourself and others. I define love as the ability to recognize another person's potential and accept them where they are without judgment, criticism, guilt, or shame, while giving them the space to embrace the complete beauty God created in them. This love also allows others to freely and openly express their true feelings rather than hide them by expressing sideways feelings instead.

True boundaries create a safe structure of guidance and discipline for the people you set them with, which does not include punishment. Athletes apply discipline to help improve their skills. True boundaries help people refine their skills around self-respect and to create safety. Proverbs 13:24, "Whoever spares the rod hates the child, but whoever loves will apply discipline," validates what the teenagers I've met with in correction institutions were saying when they talked about not feeling loved by their parents because their parents did not care enough about them to set boundaries but just let them do whatever they wanted.

Saying Yes and No with Loving Boundaries

Even though boundaries are not about pushing others away or

keeping them at a distance, it's true that one element of boundaries is about saying no. That "no" is not directed at the other person but at a specific negative behavior.

When you create true boundaries, some of the behaviors and negative patterns you are saying "no" to are:

- No, I don't want chaos any more.

- No, we aren't going to stay on autopilot in what's familiar; we're going to make a conscious effort to do better.

- No, I'm not going to be treated abusively any more.

- No, there's no longer a free ride.

- No, I will no longer accept disrespect.

- No, I won't allow you to be a person who treats yourself with disrespect by treating me and others that way.

- No, I won't settle for your being less than real.

- No, I will no longer abuse myself with negative self-talk, lies, and deceit.

- No, I won't accept excuses. (With true boundaries, there are no excuses; someone either respects the limit and chooses positive consequences or violates the limit and chooses negative consequences.)

Even more, however, true boundaries are about saying "yes." This does not mean getting others to say yes to what you want, but affirmatively and actively choosing more respectful patterns of behavior that support closer relationships. Here are some of the ways true boundaries are about saying "yes:"

- Yes, I care about and respect you enough to create boundaries that teach you how to have a safe, respectful relationship with me.

- Yes, I'm allowing us the freedom to choose our own behavior and take responsibility for the positive or negative consequences.

- Yes, I matter enough to stand up for myself.

- Yes, you matter enough to me that I'm willing to do the work of setting boundaries.

- Yes, my relationship with you is important to me and I want to keep it.

- Yes, I want the relationship to be loving, respectful, and stronger than it is now.

- Yes, I want more safety and trust for both of us.

- Yes, I would like us to learn to respect ourselves and learn to create our own true boundaries.

- Yes, I choose to respect myself and not accept disrespect from myself or others.

- Yes, I'm willing to stand up for what I believe in to create a healthier environment for both of us.

- Yes, my voice matters; I have a right to my opinions as long as they're respectful.

- Yes, your voice matters; you have a right to your opinions as long as they're respectful.

- Yes, I want each of us to be accountable for our own actions.

- Yes, I want to give us the opportunity to learn from our own mistakes and actions.

- Yes, I want both of us to learn healthier patterns in the way we relate to each other.

- Yes, I think you are competent and capable of learning the life skills necessary to take care of yourself.

- Yes, I would like us to be people who treat ourselves and others with respect.

- Yes, I think you're capable of trustworthy, respectful behavior.

- Yes, I believe your true self is loving and respectful.

- Yes, I want to honor both of us by using true boundaries to build mutual respect in our relationship.

- Yes, we both have value.

A fundamental aspect of loving and respectful boundaries is the value you have for yourself. To create true boundaries successfully, you need to understand and believe you have the right and responsibility to say both yes and no, instead of believing you passively have to accept whatever other people do around you.

Veronica was sad and anxious about what to do with her husband Fred. They had gotten into an argument six months earlier and Fred was still not talking or interacting with her. Veronica related to her counselor the many different ways she attempted to get him to start recognizing and interacting with her again to no avail.

Veronica was invited to consider setting a boundary with Fred. Veronica let Fred know she was going to honor his distance. If Fred wanted to reconnect as a couple, life would go on as usual. If Fred wanted to continue with distance in the relationship, Veronica would give Fred his space. She would stop attempting to talk with him or letting him know what was going on with their children. Veronica would not inform Fred when or where she would be going or when she would return because his actions indicated he did not want any of that sort of interaction. Additionally, Veronica would not be making his meals or washing his clothes because, again, his actions indicated he did not want her involvement with any aspect of his life.

While Veronica really wanted to reconnect with Fred, out of love and respect for herself and Fred, she went home and shared the boundary with Fred and let him have the space he was seeking. After two days of space, Fred reconnected with Veronica and they were able to reconnect as a couple.

When you set true boundaries with another person, you are not directly saying no or yes. The person the boundary is being set with is actually saying no or yes with their behavior. The love you show with true boundaries is compassion, trust, and respect for the other person by letting them have the freedom to choose either the positive or negative consequence by their behavior.

Love Expressed Through Boundaries

One of the most widely-known descriptions of love is found in the New Testament of the Bible, in 1 Corinthians 13. At first glance, this definition of love might seem to be codependent or lacking in respect for ourselves. Some of the behavior it advocates (bearing all things, for example) could be interpreted as tolerating disrespect from those around us. A closer reading, however, shows the way this view of love actually supports creating boundaries.

Cited here is the English Standard Version. It begins in verses one through three with an affirmation of love's importance:

> If I speak in the tongues of men and of angels, but have not love, I am a noisy gong or a clanging cymbal. And if I have prophetic powers, and understand all mysteries and all knowledge, and if I have all faith, so as to remove mountains, but have not love, I am nothing. If I give away all I have, and if I deliver up my body to be burned, but have not love, I gain nothing.

For true boundaries to be successful, love is critical in the process. Love invites consistent respect, consistent trust, and consistent discipline. If you are unable to care about and love yourself and the people you set the boundaries with, you will not have the commitment to follow through and maintain the boundaries in a consistent, caring, respectful, and loving fashion. Rather, you may talk about boundaries and have none.

Additionally, in verses four through seven, love is defined in terms of behavior:

> Love is patient and kind; love does not envy or boast; it is not arrogant or rude. It does not insist on its own way; it is not irritable or resentful; it does not rejoice at wrongdoing, but rejoices with the truth. Love bears all things, believes all things, hopes all things, endures all things.

Let's take a look at how boundaries relate to each of these descriptions of love:

Love is patient and kind. Patience is certainly a requirement when it comes to setting limits and following through consistently with consequences. The patience is the willingness to wait for the other person to desire and choose the positive consequence, while allowing them the permission to choose the negative consequence. Kindness is equally important. To be effective, boundaries are created with respect and consistency, not with anger or a desire to punish. When you follow through neutrally with consequences, rather than reacting with emotionally-based rewards or punishments, you take the emotion out of your interactions in a loving and respectful way. This follow-through helps fulfill the boundaries' intent, which is to increase safety, foster mutual respect, and create an environment for reflection.

Samantha and Ken's marriage had been filled with arguments and disrespect throughout their entire relationship. When Samantha sought counseling, she was desperate and didn't know what to do. She loved Ken and didn't want the relationship to end, but she could no longer handle the verbal abuse she was receiving. With some coaching, Samantha decided to establish some boundaries around the way she was treated and criticized by Ken. Samantha informed Ken, with a written boundary, that when she was being respected, she was open to engage and communicate with Ken. When Ken was being verbally abusive, controlling, and criticizing in a conversation, Samantha would create a safe distance with him. When Ken committed to respectfully reengaging, Samantha would continue with the conversation. If Samantha was disrespected again, she would create the safe distance again.

Samantha learned that Ken's pattern of disrespect was strong. Even with the persistent disrespect, Samantha kept her commitment to follow through with the boundaries she established. Samantha patiently remained emotionally disconnected from Ken's anger pattern. Initially, Ken did not seem affected by the distance. As time passed, he slowly started to shift and reflect on his behavior. Ken began recognizing and feeling the distance created by his behavior, which mattered to him because he also wanted the relationship to work. Samantha's patience in following through provided the time needed for the disrespectful pattern to change.

Love does not envy or boast. Both envy and boasting often reflect a relationship that is out of balance. When you take on the victim's role, you may become envious of the power that seems to be held by the other person. When you take on the bully's role, you may be trying to gain respect through sideways means: boasting in an attempt to create a sense of self-worth. The common thread is that both those who envy and those who boast are not comfortable with themselves and do not value and respect their true selves. When true boundaries exist, there is no need to be envious or boastful because the sideways emotions are removed from the situation and each person is equal in the relationship.

Love is not arrogant or rude. True boundaries are not created from an arrogant position of "I am better or more important than you," but from a position of strength and self-respect based on equality. They are not created with harshness and rudeness, but with language and behavior that are respectful of both the boundary creator and the boundary recipient.

Love does not insist on its own way. It may seem that setting limits is insisting on your own way. True boundaries, however, are created with respect for others as well as for yourself. They do not insist on "my way," but on a shared and equal way—a way of mutual respect intended to create safety for both parties. Boundaries are not about controlling others' behavior or making them do what you want; they are about respectfully allowing and teaching people to be responsible for their own behavior. Boundaries are created to allow recipients the free will to choose which consequence will be carried out by their actions; it truly is their choice.

Love is not irritable or resentful. When you live without boundaries, you are certainly going to experience irritation and resentment. Patterns of inconsistent punishments and rewards build anger and resentment on both sides. Calmly following through with the consequences others choose by their actions, however, neutralizes these emotions and builds mutual respect.

Connie and her sixteen-year-old daughter, Kendra, were in constant conflict over Kendra's cellphone. Connie was especially concerned about nighttime phone calls and texts interrupting her daughter's sleep. Scolding, punishments, and lectures about how much sleep teenagers need built resentment between mother and daughter and made no difference in Kendra's phone habits. Finally, Connie created a boundary. Kendra's phone charger would be kept on the kitchen counter. At 10:00 p.m. on weeknights and at her curfew time on weekends, Kendra would put her phone in the charger and leave it there until she got up the next morning. If Kendra complied with this limit, her sleep would not be interrupted and her phone would be charged and available for the next day. If she used her phone after the designated time, the next evening the phone and charger would be placed in Connie's bedroom by 9:30, and the phone would not be available to Kendra until her mother got up the next morning.

As Connie followed through calmly with the boundary, the irritation between her and Kendra over this issue gradually eased, and their relationship became more respectful.

Love does not rejoice at wrongdoing, but rejoices with the truth. "Rejoicing at wrongdoing" is an excellent description of a cycle of resentment and punishment. Rejoicing or being rewarded by wrongdoing can also describe the negative payoffs that come with a lack of boundaries. Another translation of this passage reads "*does not count up wrongdoing.*" This is an apt description of what you do when you focus on "what they did to me." When you keep score of disrespectful actions and punishments on both sides to track "wins" and "losses," you are nursing your resentment and helping to keep yourself and others stuck in familiar disrespectful behaviors.

"Rejoicing with the truth," in contrast, describes being willing to look at an existing pattern of disrespect and taking ownership of your part, which helps create emotional freedom. It means taking responsibility for your actions and your part in that pattern instead of merely blaming the other person.

When you create consistency in following through, there is no need to keep score. Connie's follow-through with her boundary about Kendra's cell phone wasn't about winning or losing, but about consistently allowing Kendra the choice of which consequence she wished to receive. If Kendra should consistently choose the negative consequence, that still would not be a "defeat" for Connie or a sign that the boundary was not working. It would indicate that a slight increase in the negative consequence might be necessary to get Kendra's attention and build her desire to follow through with the positive consequence.

Love bears all things, believes all things, hopes all things, endures all things. This is the passage that could seem to support codependent behavior and even directly contradict creating boundaries. "Bearing all things and enduring all things" might be interpreted as allowing yourself to be treated with disrespect and tolerating abuse.

Here is another way to look at it: Love—for both yourself and others—is what gives you the strength and willingness to "bear and endure" the hard work and emotional pain of building stronger relationships. Love helps you learn to value yourself and create boundaries to change disrespectful patterns that harm your relationships. "Believing and hoping all things" is a willingness to accept that change is possible. It is also a willingness to see both yourself and others as worthy of respect and capable of changing.

This passage ultimately speaks about the patience necessary to follow through consistently with boundaries. It is especially necessary when the boundary is first established, since the boundary will be challenged until consistency is established and maintained. When you become impatient, you tend to get upset, and the sideways feelings of anger start to show up in many different ways. The patience is what allows you to act with love, faith, hope, and consistency, rather than anger and resentment.

§§§§§

Creating true boundaries and consistently following through with them is an act of love for ourselves and the people around us. This love is felt through a decrease in the arguments, fights, sideways feelings, and insecurity that occur when true boundaries are not present. It is also felt in the increased respect, consistency, and positive attention that come with true boundaries.

- *True Boundaries give us faith* by the consistency and stability they create, which helps build more trusting relationships.

- *True Boundaries give us hope* by allowing trust to build, which helps both parties to be open to new possibilities of respect in their relationship.

- *True Boundaries create love* by creating free choice.

- *True Boundaries create safe space* for freedom of choice, speaking truth, and feeling our true feelings.

Choosing the positive or negative consequence with no anger, resentment, guilt, or shame allows for more consistent choosing of positive consequences, which creates the respect, safety, and love we all desire.

Chapter Nine Reflections

In relationships you want to love and be loved, yet your interactions many times demonstrate behaviors that are not loving. When love exists, there is safety, respect, acceptance, true feelings, connectedness, and God. All of this occurs because you have and are given choices in which you take ownership.

As you work to establish true boundaries in your relationships, list the areas where you are starting to take ownership rather than blaming the other person as you may have done in the past.

_____

_____

_____

List the ways these boundaries are helping you realize more fully that you matter.

_____

_____

_____

List the ways these boundaries are helping with love, patience, and kindness for you.

_____

_____

_____

List the areas in which anger, resentment, jealousy, blame, irritability, shortness, or getting even have decreased with the successful creation and testing of boundaries.

_____

_____

_____

LIVING WITH TRUE BOUNDARIES

"It is necessary, and even vital, to set standards for
your life and the people you allow in it."

— Mandy Hale

This book's introduction uses the metaphor of a basketball game to describe the chaos that results from a lack of boundaries. At first glance, an athletic event may not seem to have much to do with love and relationships. Yet love is one of the fundamental reasons sports and games even exist. While it may be described in other terms, like passion or energy or having fun, one emotion that drives people to commit time and energy to athletics is love. Love of using one's talent and skill. Love of competition that pushes one to excel. Love of teammates and coaches. Love of the sport itself.

At the same time, just think of the conflicting goals and needs of the various participants in a basketball game. Each team wants to win. Individual players want to win, to play well, to help other members of their team play well, or perhaps to outshine their team members. In addition to the spirit of competition, all the players have their individual personalities, relationships with each other, difficulties to overcome, and passion for the game. That adds up to a great deal of energy and a high potential for conflict.

Without rules and structure, that energy and passion can easily transform a game into a riot filled with anger, fights, and injuries, just as it plays out in relationships with no true boundaries. The game's rules and structure serve as boundaries to contain players' energy and channel their passion toward the constructive goal of playing the game well. The boundaries help keep players safe, help them behave with respect toward each other even within the competition of the game, and give them the opportunity to use their skills to the utmost while providing entertainment for the spectators and having fun. The boundaries make it possible for players to do all they can to win, and yet, at the end of the game, shake hands and walk off the court with respect for each other as competitors.

Day-to-day life in our families and workplaces doesn't usually have the same high energy and competitiveness as an athletic event. Yet some of those same dynamics of competition, conflicting goals, and passion operate within families, workplaces, and other relationships.

True boundaries, therefore, are crucial to ensure our closest, most loving relationships foster respect and safety.

Emma, like most three-year-olds, didn't appreciate having limits on her behavior or hearing the word "no." Her mother, Marissa, did quite well at setting clear boundaries and consequences with her. Following through, however, was a challenging process that too often fell apart into tears, fits, anger, and punishments.

Then Emma's great-aunt Renee came to live with the family. With plenty of experience dealing with small children, as well as a level of emotional detachment, it was easier for her not to respond to Emma's tears and fits. Renee's example and support helped Marissa more consistently follow through with consequences in a pleasant, matter-of-fact way.

Within a few weeks, much of the time Emma was respecting limits in the same matter-of-fact way. One evening she brought her mother a book, ready to start their bedtime routine. "Are your toys picked up and put away?" Marissa asked. Emma scowled and started to argue. When Marissa said nothing, Emma stopped arguing and ran off to toss her toys into their basket. She came back with a big smile. "I listened!" she told her mother proudly. Then she settled into Marissa's lap to enjoy the book.

Emma was learning not just to honor boundaries, but to honor herself. As the adults in her life set clear limits and followed through with consequences in an emotionally neutral way, they communicated to Emma that she could be trusted to choose her own behavior. The relationships shifted away from power struggles with "winners" and "losers." Instead, the true boundaries encouraged Emma to choose responses that helped her appreciate her own competence and fostered her respect for herself.

Creating true boundaries with a boss, spouse, or parent may feel much riskier than setting boundaries with young children. If you begin setting boundaries that change the way you interact with a preschooler, you have a great deal to gain and little to lose. The child can't fire you, end the relationship, or physically harm you. The stakes may seem much higher with adults, especially those you perceive as having power over you.

Yet true boundaries work much the same way for other adults as they do for children. This is true whether those adults are peers, employees, supervisors, parents, grown children, or spouses. When you set appropriate limits, establish clear positive and negative consequences, and follow through in a respectful, calm way, you provide a powerful example of mutual respect.

If you are frustrated, fearful, or feel taken advantage of or not heard in your closest relationships, true boundaries can make a significant difference. So I urge you to take the risk to create one small boundary you can successfully follow through with. Then another one, and another, moving on to larger issues as you build your confidence. It is worth the effort. You have nothing to lose except chaos, resentment, and tension. What you have to gain is increased communication, energy, calmness, and cooperation based on respect. And remember, that respect enhances relationships in four ways: your respect for yourself, others' respect for you, your respect for others, and their respect for themselves.

Without boundaries, even when we love each other, we can all too easily hurt, bully, and resent each other. Love is the foundation that binds us together as families; boundaries provide a structure to help us express that love with respect and safety for ourselves and each other. True boundaries allow each of us the freedom to be our best selves.

Chapter Ten Reflections

List the boundaries you have successfully created, implemented, tested, and established.

List the steps you took to create the successes.

_____

_____

_____

Take time to reflect on what you are willing to do differently with the boundaries that were not successful.

_____

_____

_____

List ways you can celebrate your successes with true boundaries to help and encourage more successes.

_____

_____

_____

A FINAL NOTE

EMPOWERING YOUR LIFE
WITH CHOICES

After reading this book and completing the reflections, what is your next step? How do you want to use what you have learned to create positive change in your life? Who are you hoping to partner with for support and objectivity with the implementation of the boundaries you intend to put in place?

Creating true boundaries can be challenging because almost everyone you intend to set boundaries with has not experienced this way of interacting before. The chapter reflections have allowed you the opportunity to create written boundaries with positive and negative consequences. Achieving your goals begins with the emotionally small boundaries. It is important to start small and work up to more emotionally charged boundaries. Once you have successes, they will help create more confidence in yourself and the person you are setting the boundary with.

To help create success with the boundaries, I invite you to consider whom in your life you can share your boundaries with who will be objective and supportive. Invite them to be a sounding board on these boundaries and to challenge you in ways to make them emotionally neutral and more effective. Additionally, I invite you to be that person for them as well. To help successfully move forward with boundaries, get a pen or pencil, and in the ten exercise lines below, write out the ten actions you intend to take in the next three months to have successful boundaries become part of your life.

Write ten boundary actions you will commit to over the next three months.

1. _____

2. _____

3. _____

4. _____

5. _____

6. _____

7. _____

8. _____

9. _____

10. _____

Use this book as a study guide, going back to the reflection questions as much as you want. The reflection questions can be used over and over as the desire for additional boundaries becomes apparent.

In this book, you learned that boundaries have three components: a limit, positive and negative consequences that directly relate to the limit, and follow through. Additionally, you learned you may not have true boundaries because you were not taught what a true boundary is or what it would even look like. You learned that true boundaries are difficult to implement because fear, ignorance, negative payoffs, and codependency impede their success.

This book was designed to help you learn what a real boundary is and the necessary steps to create successful outcomes with their implementation. Creating true boundaries takes time and work. If you are willing to invest the time and effort necessary, relationships can change for the positive.

If you create and follow through with these boundaries in your life, you will start to truly change your life, the way you see yourself, the way others see you, the way you treat yourself, and the way others treat you. This change creates the trust, safety, and respect you desire and deserve.

Now that you have read my book, I encourage you to let me know what was helpful and what was confusing so I can improve this book for its next edition and help you and other readers better. My email is jetsond@yahoo.com.

I hope you are empowered with great success as you develop and implement your boundaries. Thank you for your interest in wanting to create a better world starting with relationships in your life.

Sincerely,

Dave Jetson

ABOUT THE AUTHOR

Dave Jetson, MS, is a licensed professional counselor. In 2003, he earned his MS in counseling at South Dakota State University, graduating summa cum laude. Since then, he has been providing individual therapy as well as facilitating groups and workshops. He offers many different therapeutic techniques to help clients connect with themselves. After training in and experiencing various types of therapy, he has embraced intuitive experiential therapy because it is so effective in healing emotional trauma. He works with clients individually, provides relationship and family counseling, and offers experiential group therapy and workshops. He is a pioneer in offering both individual and group experiential therapy via Internet video conferencing.

The workshops Dave has created include Freedom from Negative Self-Talk, Sexuality and Relationships, Personal Connections in the Wilderness, Codependency, Connecting with your Inner Child, Body Language, Financial Therapy, Love, Money and Couples, and Financial Codependency. His Financial Recovery workshops feature experiential exercises using clients' real money.

Dave has given talks and facilitated workshops across the United States as well as in Panama, Chile, and Australia. His work has been featured in *Self* magazine and *The Journal of Traditional Eastern Health & Fitness*, and he has been cited in *The Wall Street Journal*.

Dave's first book, *Finding Emotional Freedom*, was published in February of 2013. It describes the path to deep recovery from codependency through intuitive experiential therapy. This deep emotional work accesses both the conscious and unconscious parts of the brain to provide powerful, lasting recovery from emotional trauma. It combines current brain research with Dave's observation and experience with clients to explain for both professionals and non-professionals why this therapy is so effective. An excerpt from *Finding Emotional Freedom* is at the end of this book. *Setting True Boundaries* is his second book, with more in the works.

Today, Dave lives in South Dakota with his wife. He has three dogs, a German Shepherd (large), a Springer Spaniel (medium), and a Shih Tzu (small) he walks each day in the woods. In his spare time, he enjoys hiking, biking, meditating, checking on his beehive, and playing games with his kids and grandchildren.

EXCERPT FROM FINDING EMOTIONAL FREEDOM BY DAVE JETSON

Keep reading for an excerpt from Dave's previous book, *Finding Emotional Freedom: Access the Truth Your Brain Already Knows*. If you want to learn more about recovery from codependency and deep emotional trauma, you can find this book in both print and ebook editions from major online retailers and bookstores.

Finding Emotional Freedom:

Access the Truth Your Brain Already Knows

This book provides a path out of emotional trauma to the emotional freedom that is our birthright. Dave uses intuitive experiential therapy to help clients access both the mind and the heart. In this book, he combines current brain research with his years of experience to offer a compelling method of deep recovery and transformation.

Introduction

Scars. They are visible reminders of old wounds. Like most of us, you probably have a few scars and remember where many of them came from. The place on your knee that you skinned so badly the time you wrecked your bike. The mark on your temple that's a reminder of having chicken pox when you were four. The crooked line on your arm where the neighbor's cat scratched you when you tried to dress it up in doll's clothes.

Most of the time, our physical scars are so insignificant that we pay little attention to them. Others, however, are hard to ignore. Some of us may have scars left by more serious trauma such as severe burns, car accidents, falls, illnesses, or surgeries. Such major wounds can leave us not only with disfiguring scars, but with lasting disabilities that inter-fere with our ability to lead active, normal lives.

We all have emotional scars as well as physical scars. Many of these emotional scars are as insignificant as our physical reminders of childhood mishaps. We hardly notice them. More severe emotional wounds, however, can have as much long-term impact as severe phys-ical wounds. These wounds, or emotional traumas, may be caused by growing up in families that are dysfunctional because of abuse associ-ated with abandonment, addictions, mental illness, anger, or fear. They may be the result of neglect or physical, sexual, or emotional abuse. They may result from losses such as the death of a parent. Emotional trauma can leave us dysfunctional, in pain, and disabled to the point of being unable to live normal lives. Yet because emotional wounds are not as immediately visible as physical ones, their after-effects may cause us to live in misery for years without even knowing why.

Those who live with unhealed emotional wounds may feel hurt, betrayed, angry, or resentful a lot of the time. We may feel like victims. We may feel powerless. We may tell ourselves we don't deserve better lives than the limited or unhappy ones we have. We may abuse our-selves through addictions such as alcoholism, tobacco use, drug use, workaholism, sex, or overeating. We may hide ourselves from life and from other people with the destructive overuse of distractions such as television or video games. We may abuse both ourselves and those around us with anger.

Serious emotional trauma attacks our deepest, truest selves. It drives us to hide who we are and deprives us of our authentic voices. We may find ways to live with the wounds from such trauma: to hide them, to pretend they don't exist, and even to heal them on the surface. Yet beneath that superficial healing often lie ugly, festering emotional sores that cause us enduring pain.

When we have been wounded, we subconsciously build inner emotional walls to protect ourselves from those we believe might harm us. The parts of our brains that deal with emotions create those barriers with nothing but our best interests in mind. Unfortunately, the walls lock away our true feelings so thoroughly that those feelings become hidden even from ourselves. Eventually, the walls isolate us emotionally until they become our prisons.

The work of pioneering psychotherapists like Virginia Satir and Dr. Bessel A. van der Kolk has shown that experiential therapy can help people break down these emotional walls to access their hidden feelings and heal emotional trauma. The more I used this type of therapy with clients and observed the patterns they presented as they explored their deep emotional issues, the more I realized that a deeper understanding of the brain would be helpful. What I discovered is that research in neuroscience is beginning to confirm the value of experiential work by showing us how the brain processes traumatic experiences.

Some of this research shows that the efforts our brains make to protect us by hiding our true feelings create learned patterns of conflicting responses. Essentially, our brains are in conflict with themselves, which only creates more trauma. Experiential therapy allows our brains to reset these patterns and create lasting change. As information on the complexity of the brain continues to be discovered, neuroscience will help us explain even more fully what happens when we are willing to explore our core emotional issues.

When we are willing to take the emotional risks of searching beyond our brain's protective barriers, we are able to heal our deep emotional wounds. Exposing and healing our deep emotional pain is not something we can do with the traditional tools of talk therapy. Behavioral/cognitive counseling, which focuses on the conscious, thinking functions of our brains, can help us make changes and manage our lives better. For many people, this is enough. Yet for anyone with deep emotional trauma, that type of work does not go deep enough for healing.

For those who have deep, disabling emotional wounds, healing requires the equivalent of emotional surgery. The kinds of counseling most effective for such surgery, which have worked for me as well as many of my clients, are experiential and intuitive therapy. Experiential therapy uses many different interactive methods to help people connect with feelings they have hidden from themselves. It is a powerful force for lasting change because it connects both the mind and the heart. The intuitive therapy that I practice is a form of experiential work that goes a step further, focusing on what clients' body language reveals about their deep emotions. Throughout the book I use the term intuitive/experiential therapy to refer to these processes.

Exploring our innermost selves through this form of therapy is one of the hardest and most rewarding things any of us can ever do. It takes trust, commitment, and a great deal of courage. In exchange, it offers powerful, life-changing transformation. The benefit of intuitive emotional therapy is, at a minimum, freedom from emotional and often physical pain. It won't erase problems from our lives, but it helps us to live at peace with ourselves and those around us. Even more, it allows us to begin living fully and freely as the persons we really are. It allows us to rediscover our authentic selves, know and speak our truth with the full power of our emotional voices, and regain the emotional freedom that is our birthright

It's my hope that this book will offer possibilities for change to anyone who is suffering from emotional wounds and wants to find a way to heal them. If you are among those looking for such healing, I encourage you to seek help from a therapist trained in intuitive/experiential therapy. The book is for you if any of the following is true in your life:

- Your childhood was marked by abandonment, neglect, and abuse in one or more of the following ways: physical, verbal, emotional, sexual, religious, illness, ritual, abandonment, or disability.

- You want to live a full, authentic, happy life, but you have sabotaged your own efforts to do so.

- You suffer from physical illnesses and pain that may be rooted in emotional pain.

- You have an internal sense of living a lie.

- You have an internal feeling of being stuck and trapped, without knowing why, and you don't see any way out.

- Treatment programs have had little or no success with your addiction.

- You repeat destructive patterns in relationships and in your work that have a negative impact on your life.

- You have read and followed the recommendations of self-help books, participated in support groups, and gone to counseling, but with little long-term success.

- You haven't been able to make lasting changes.

- You have little or no emotional voice, and you're not even sure what an emotional voice is.

- You continually beat yourself up with negative self-talk.

Intuitive/experiential therapy is based on several fundamental precepts:

1. The ultimate truth is "the truth will set you free." The key to deep emotional healing is connecting with our emotional truth. We need to learn how to listen to ourselves to know what our truth is. Once we can allow ourselves to feel our truth, we can speak our truth clearly and directly. We need someone to support us as we learn to listen to ourselves and to listen to our truth. This support

and listening are crucial parts of the counselor's role as well as the role of safe, close friends.

2. Experiencing intense emotions such as fear, anger, guilt, and sadness can be frightening. Yet when we dig deep enough to uncover our deepest, authentic emotions, we learn that they will never harm ourselves, other people, or things of importance. Our core true selves and true feelings are our connection with God, ultimately gentle, loving, and respectful of ourselves and others.

3. There is incredible power in authenticity. When our words, actions, thoughts, body language, and true feelings all line up, we are communicating as our authentic selves. Then we can be clearly heard even when we whisper.

4. Every emotional trauma has been created with the help of someone or something else, so healing has to be done with the help of someone else. The most effective helper or guide is a therapist trained in this type of work. Such a professional has the skills and experience to create a safe emotional space for clients to explore their deepest and most painful emotions. The most essential qualities in helpers or guides, however, are their willingness to give us permission to be our true selves, their willingness to listen intently while not judging, their ability to stay with us during the frightening and difficult parts of the journey, and their experience of making a similar journey themselves. Even therapists with strong skills and training, if they have not done their own emotional healing at this level, will not be able to guide clients' journeys any deeper than they have gone on that issue themselves.

5. Looking at the past matters. True, we can't change the past. We can't make the trauma that has damaged us go away. What we can do is allow ourselves to heal that damage. We can explore and heal the unresolved feelings that have had such a negative and limiting

effect on all our decisions in the present.

6. Change is a choice. Recovery begins when we feel a certain level of emotional safety and decide for ourselves that we're ready to start the journey. For one reason or another, we realize that the pain of staying the same no longer seems safer or easier than the effort of making a change. That decision point comes in different ways for different people, but it is always an individual choice. Therapists, spouses, and family members cannot force or manipulate us into lasting change until we are ready to choose recovery.

7. The transformational power of recovery does not change who we are. Instead, it allows us to access the truth about ourselves that our brains have always known—that we are fundamentally loving, caring, and respectful. It frees us to live authentically as the unique selves we were always meant to be.

This is not a self-help book. It can give you some insights and awareness, but merely reading it is not likely to be enough to help you change your life. Deep intuitive work like this cannot be done on your own. This book shows you a path you can choose that will lead to healing and recovery. The path to deep emotional healing is difficult, frightening, sometimes dark, and very rewarding. Following it requires courage, trust, and deep love for and commitment to yourself. You can't walk it by yourself, but you don't have to. This book will show you how to start and where to find guides to walk it with you.